The Home

The Home

*A Memoir of Growing Up
in an Orphanage*

RICHARD McKENZIE

BasicBooks
A Division of HarperCollins*Publishers*

Designed by Elliott Beard

Library of Congress Cataloging-in-Publication Data
McKenzie, Richard B.
    The home : a memoir of growing up in an orphanage / by Richard
McKenzie.
        p.   cm.
    ISBN 0-465-03068-8
    1. Orphanages—North Carolina—History.   2. Orphans—North
Carolina—Biography.   I. Title.
    HV990.N8M35   1996
    362.7'32'092—dc20
    [B]   95-37831
                                                             CIP

96 97 98 99 ❖/RRD 9 8 7 6 5 4 3

For Kathryn

CONTENTS

ACKNOWLEDGMENTS

WRITING BOOKS HAS BEEN A LARGE PART OF MY WORK AS AN ADULT, but completing this book has been an emotional trip back in time and into my soul. I was able to make that trip with the help of others who provided guidance. My wife, Karen, gave me invaluable assessments of and suggestions on every draft of the manuscript. My editors at Basic Books, Jo Ann Miller and Linda Carbone, pressed me to fill in many of the descriptive and emotional details of the stories and stream-lined the flow of the words. I am also indebted to a number of friends and colleagues who took the time to read various drafts of the book and to offer their advice: Candace Allen, Tinamarie Bernard, Henry and Kay Bridges, Douglas Byrd, Amrita Danierre, Donald Frazier, Jim and Lane Kiser, Dwight Lee,

Roger Lovette, Catherine McFarlane, Paige Moore, Cynthia Morris, Christine Moseley, Lawton Nesbit, Victoria Ongie, Kay Reimler, Judy and Joseph Rosener, Robin Schupp, and Donna Specter. I have very much appreciated the support given by the Earhart Foundation and the Lyde and Harry Bradley Foundation to undertake research on topics related to this book. And, finally, I am eternally indebted to the girls and boys of The Home, with whom I took the trip of a lifetime.

All four of my children have been very important in my life, and I've taken great pleasure in dedicating my books to each of them, one at a time. At the time this book was written, my daughter Kathryn was six years old, a charmer with eyes as blue as her grandfather's and a smile as expansive as her grandmother's. I dedicate this book with love to her because she is what you read between the lines. As I wrote this book, I thought a lot about Kathryn. I saw her as a product of the past that is told here and as a link to the distant future that her mother and I can share with her in spirit if not always in body. I thought a lot about the contrast between the childhood I had and the childhood she is having, the latter attributable in no small measure to the former. To understand fully why The Home remains of central importance to me, you would have to meet Kathryn and see her look into the future, full of hope and promise.

—September 1995

PROLOGUE

AT THE START OF THE MOVIE *ANNIE*, MISS HANNIGAN—THE decadent, overbearing housemother—wonders in obvious exasperation, "Why any kid would want to be an orphan is beyond me."

The stark contrast between that movie's version of orphanage life and the life Annie came to know with her wealthy adoptive father, Daddy Warbucks, convinced many moviegoers that Miss Hannigan was right: indeed, no one would ever want to be an orphan. Social critics continue to paint dreadful pictures of life in homes for children, suggesting that bringing back orphanages would be disastrous. According to virtually all child-care professionals, the orphanages that dotted America's social landscape for the first two-thirds of this century served only to damage the children in their care in all important regards — emotionally, educationally, and economically.

A funny thing has happened in the emerging debate over what to do with the parentless, neglected, abused, or abandoned children in our midst: no one has thought to ask orphans themselves, the children who were there, what they think about their years in the orphanage.

I've spent a lifetime quietly listening to people disparage orphanages as cold and loveless institutions filled with pitiful children longing to be adopted. I've argued with "experts" whose ideas have no place in the debate about how to help the least fortunate children among us. I know because I was there. I grew up with two hundred girls and boys in North Carolina in the 1950s, and nearly all of us are proud of our upbringing — and thankful for it!

In my early childhood years, before going to The Home (which is what we called our orphanage), I was given to running the streets of Raleigh, North Carolina. My mother died when I was ten, and my father's alcoholism left him unable to care for my brother and me. Few of the children at the orphanage we were sent to were true orphans — that is, with both parents dead — but close to two-thirds were missing one parent. Many came from homes broken by poverty, divorce, abuse, and neglect. All were disadvantaged in one or more ways, but few were severely troubled emotionally. The average age of the children who arrived at The Home in the 1930s, 1940s, and 1950s was between seven and eight years old. The average length of stay was ten years, or, generally speaking, until they finished high school. Beginning in the mid-1950s, we were all given a chance to get a college education; what we could not pay from our wages and savings was covered by donations from individuals and churches to The Home.

But life in The Home was no picnic. We got two baths and changes of clothes a week; we went to school barefoot until late November; we went to bed in unheated "sleeping porches"; we worked long, hard hours on the farm and in the carpentry, plumbing, and printing shops; and we went without a lot, not the least of which were the hugs and the personal encouragement other children take for granted. In return we got structure and stability. We got security in the knowledge that The Home would always be there, no mean advantage for children whose families had failed them. And we got fifteen hundred acres of pastures and woods, and dozens of brothers and sisters.

And what of the people who cared for us? Critics harbor fears that such workers had no more concern for their charges than Miss Hannigan had for hers. But those critics have never had the good fortune of meeting Mr. Shanes or Miss Winfield, who, despite their lack of formal training in psychology or child care, devoted their lives to making sure that we learned (albeit reluctantly and imperfectly) the difference between right and wrong.

Critics would like the public to believe that those of us who were brought up in orphanages were throttled by the experience. True, some homes were bad places. True, some children who went through The Home did not benefit from the experience; some may still have emotional scars. However, most of us have charged on. In many ways, we represent the best of what this country is about: plumbers and nurses, ministers and managers, teachers and baggage handlers—good, well-meaning Americans who have answered the call to rise above expectations.

I now live a continent away and a world apart from that orphanage in rural North Carolina. I make my home in urban Southern California and my living as an economics professor. I have written many books and articles about issues in my professional sphere, but this book has been very different for me. It has been a profound personal journey, one of whose many benefits was that it stoked my curiosity about how the children I was raised with, as well as those in other orphanages, turned out. I spent the better part of a year looking through records and undertaking a survey of the thousand or so living alumni of The Home. (The details of the findings are reported in Richard B. McKenzie, "Orphanages: Did They Throttle the Children in Their Care?" *The Public Interest* [Spring 1996].)

One of the surprising things I found out was that during World War II, when the military was turning down close to 40 percent of draftees from the general population, it rejected a scant 1.4 percent of the boys from The Home. I was also astonished to learn that the hundreds of fellow alumni who responded to my survey (at an average age of sixty-six) surpassed their counterarts in the general white population at every rung of the educational ladder, up through advanced degrees.

Many critics worry that orphans are bound to repeat the destitution they knew in their families. Wrong again: in 1994, the orphans from The Home had a median income (the income of the person in the middle of the distribution) from one-fifth to three-fifths higher (depending on age group) than the general population. And, compared to their counterparts, the alumni report relatively low rates of emotional difficulty, incarceration, and need for public assistance.

In fact, former orphans as a group indicate a far more positive attitude toward life than the average American. The following question has been posed to a large number of Americans practically every year since 1957: "Taking all things together, how would you say things are going these days?" Twice as many orphans chose "very happy" as a reply, compared to the general population. Only one orphan for every three people in the general population chose "not too happy."

Contrary to what might be supposed, then, these orphans showed an overwhelming preference for their way of growing up to the next best alternative. When asked whether they would rather have grown up in foster care, over 90 percent said no and less than 1 percent said yes (with the rest uncommitted). When asked whether they would rather have grown up with the available members of their own families, over 80 percent said no and 10 percent said yes (the rest were not able to say).

I also asked them to indicate how they evaluated their care and experiences at their homes. Nearly 90 percent rated their experiences as "very favorable" or "somewhat favorable," with the rest having mixed reactions (although a number of them still indicated a preference for the way they grew up). Just over 1 percent had "somewhat unfavorable" or "very unfavorable" experiences.

Although they had advantages other children did not have, these former orphans were not reared in the lap of high-priced care. The cost per child around 1950—covering housing, recreation, supervision, and basic amenities (after allowing for the work the children did on the farms and in the shops)—was less than $3,000 annually, in 1995 dollars! When education and general administration costs are added, the per-child cost reached no higher than $5,000 a year. And few alumni complained in the survey about the lack of basic amenities. Many attributed their success to the education, values, discipline, and work ethic instilled in them during their childhood years at the orphanage. For kids who supposedly grew up the hard way, these children have clearly outpaced their counterparts in the general population. The many good people who worked at The Home knew how to break the cycles of poverty, abuse, and neglect we had known before coming there.

To be sure, the results of my survey are limited, since respondents were not drawn randomly from the national population of former orphans. They are from one home, the one that nurtured me. But I can tell you that my findings are being duplicated by responses from alumni of other homes for children. Even after allowing for some upward bias in the findings, the results still seriously undermine some of the critics' most cherished and sweeping negative assessments of life in America's orphanages.

When I look back at my life at The Home, I can see why so many of us turned out well (although everyone who went through The Home understands that others might be surprised). It is my hope that by sharing my memories of daily life in a home for children, I will help readers understand why an orphanage can be a refuge and a source of inspiration and why the overwhelming majority of those who spent their childhoods there can look back on them with fondness and gratitude.

The tales I relate here are at times sad and at other times uplifting. They are at all times faithfully told, even when personal traumas are involved. I have changed the names to protect privacy and I may have inadvertently misplaced some of the details in time, but everything reported in these pages happened. This can only be my story, however. If all the children's stories could be written, many of the impressions and emotions would be different. But, I am certain, one theme would emerge: life at The Home was a vast improvement on the lives we had known before arriving there.

For most of us, The Home was a place to change course. It offered a set of experiences that were life-focusing. It gave us constraints, direction, purpose, and inspiration. The Home in rural North Carolina is no longer a place, although a few of the old buildings still stand. Now it represents a state of mind, a past we cannot forget and would not if we could. In my remembered experiences at The Home lie a partial explanation for why the children who spent their days and nights there have done what they have done, and will continue to do, in life.

Most of the children who grew up at The Home, which opened its doors in 1891, would not, as I have said, have wanted to continue on the path they had been before. Myles remembers what it was like to roam the streets of his hometown, getting into trouble and finding food where he could. Rebecca remembers The Home as the first place she ever used an inside flush toilet. Neal first knew there what it was like to have something more than bread and water for dinner. Many recall being grossly neglected or beaten or simply abandoned before finding themselves at The Home. Nevertheless, some, even those who arrived very young, as young as two, still fight the personal pain of their very early days there, when they first became aware that they had been discarded.

Obviously, if any of us had been given a choice between growing up with Ozzie and Harriet or in The Home, we would surely have taken the former. But our families had failed us, and we didn't want to take the risk that another family would do the same. Virtually all of us today shudder at the foster-care option. Foster families cannot offer children a sense of permanence, and the children can never be sure whether foster parents are taking them in as a personal mission or just for the money. The dominant emotion of those of us brought up in The Home who return each year to homecoming is neither hostility nor regret but sheer gratitude for all the positive attributes of institutional care we benefited from that are rarely acknowledged: security, stability, and permanence. In offering those advantages, The Home set boundaries for us within which we could create our own little successes—from building forts in the woods to playing sports to nurturing younger children—and on which we could build our larger successes after leaving The Home.

With all the current talk about family values, we must remember that there are families that value very little, least of all their children. Some families are worse for children than even the worst of institutions.

Miss Hannigan, you should have asked a real orphan, not the ones cast in Hollywood or Washington. Life in a home for children is not perfect. If children's homes are ever reinstituted, reforms are obviously needed. But it is my strong conviction that they should be a viable option for children. Those of us who were there share an array of experiences that children from many families—the traditional ones and the publicly supported variants—can only envy.

The greatest wealth a man may acquire
Is the wisdom he gains from living.

Sometimes out of small beginnings
Come the forces that shape a whole life.

—So Dear to My Heart,
a film by Walt Disney (1948)

I

SUMMER DRUMS

THE BEAT OF A LONE DRUMMER IN A CORTEGE HAS ALWAYS haunted me: *Rat-a-tat-tat, rat-a-tat-tat. Rat-a-tat-tat, rat-a-tat . . . tat.* It brings back the sights and smells and sounds of a childhood horror: *Rat-a-tat-tat, rat-a-tat-tat.* It reminds me of where I came from and of the emotional odyssey I've made.

I never understood that my private horror was shared by the other boys involved until the mid-1980s, when I met my old friend Dooley for lunch in Planesville, a small town five miles north of The Home. He had been one of my closest buddies at the orphanage, but I had not seen him in years. Back then, Dooley was smaller than the other boys, with black hair and something of a beaked nose, but an expansive smile. At lunch,

I saw in him how much I had aged. His full beard was beginning to gray; his stomach showed signs of sagging. He had not lost his devious chuckle, though, the one that said, "What can we get in to next?"

We covered the usual topics of our lives since leaving The Home—college, marriage, children, divorce—but we kept coming back to what we remembered most, our fond memories of The Home.

We lived lives there that Huck Finn would recognize. Work started early and ended late: hauling hay, hoeing cornfields into rows that stretched beyond the hills, milking cows while half asleep at dawn, cleaning out the barns (and dumping the cow dung in the proverbial brick shithouse).

But stretched out before us we also had fifteen hundred acres of unspoiled woods, creeks, pastures, cliffs, and old forts made by boys who had been there before us. I walked those woods endlessly in my free time, and can still remember every twist and turn in the paths I followed and every rock in the dams I made. I remember the woods and back roads as places of escape and freedom to explore and build and find a measure of inner peace. I and the other two hundred boys and girls at The Home dreamed a lot, and we had good places to do it.

Dooley and I laughed, recalling the times we had made Tarzan swings of rope and vines across ravines in remote corners of the woods, explored caves, built our own forts for future boys to discover, and, when we were older, found romance in the leaves.

Then the inevitable question arose: "What is your worst memory?" Without hesitation, we both said together, "Lady," instantly calling to mind that morning at the dairy barn when the drums beat and a measure of our childhood innocence was lost.

Once again I heard the beats of those makeshift drums pounding in my head. *Rat-a-tat-tat, rat-a-tat-tat. Rat-a-tat-tat, rat-a-tat . . . tat.*

They were never in unison, the two young boys rapping sticks on wooden crates. A small group of us—Dooley, CJ, Digger, Conner, Wiley, Mooney, Animal, Chandler, and a few others—set out for a coming-of-age ritual that would turn into something unspeakable.

I remember the sun was bright that morning in 1954, but it was still too early to be hot. The mood was somber: our task was a disquieting one for boys who were a year or so shy of puberty but out to prove their manhood (yet again). The drums were the tops of peach crates, which were always around, given the acres and acres of peach and apple orchards whose fruit we picked each summer and fall. The crates were tall and flimsy, funnel-shaped, with woven slats and tops that closed over the edges. The makeshift drums hung by baling twine around two boys' necks.

They started up the rat-a-tat beats on the dirt path just outside the milk room of the white dairy barn, whose paint was fading and curling. The beats were intended to announce a march to a wooded area a couple of hundred yards behind the barn. Exactly when the other boys picked up the fact that those drumbeats signaled an execution is hard to say, but that was the intent, as it had been a number of times before.

The victim that day was a dearly loved collie, who for several years had shown us love by her devotion to us and to her puppies. She had a litter as frequently as nature would permit, given that wild dogs always roamed the perimeter of the pastures that extended beyond the distant hilltops. We kept some of her puppies, gave others to folks in the area, and did away with the rest.

Lady had been our Lassie, loyal and spry but calm, giving, spirited, loving. Although smaller than the Lassie of film and television, she had similar coloring: white down the nose and chest and on the soft underbelly, golden brown everywhere else. Both Dooley and I still remember how much we loved that dog, and how much she loved us. We remember her hugs, her licks to the cheek. We have forgotten the nature and names of the other dogs who came our way then, but we will never forget Lady and what she went through.

Lady's misfortune was to have come down with a severe case of mange, which could not be treated; veterinarians were called to The Home only for the farm animals, not the pets. Over time, she had lost her beauty and become bone-thin, sickly, weak. Her coat was dull, not glistening the way it had been in her prime. She could no longer carry her head high.

She had to be destroyed, as had so many other of our pets, or so we thought. In those days and in that part of the country, pets with problems were pets that were destroyed. In rural North Carolina, miles from the nearest town, dogs were practically everywhere, and most had reverted to their predomestication look: thin, short-haired, fearful.

There were always pets around the barns. We used to find dens of puppies and kittens tucked away in the red dirt banks of hillsides in remote corners of the woods and make new homes for them in the haylofts. I always used to wonder whether wild mother dogs felt emotions on returning to their empty dens, or whether they knew when one or two of the litter were miss-ing. I wondered whether the puppies felt the pain of being taken from their mothers to be cared for in a totally alien place by aliens, which we must have seemed to them.

The pets we took, of course, were not allowed in the cottages and dining hall that spanned The Home's main campus up the hill, just far enough away from the dairy barns to keep the farm smells on campus to a minimum. Most of them were lean. When puppies and kittens were young, there was no problem. All we had to do was squeeze a little extra from the cows. When they got older, we shared the scraps from our plates.

We often made pets of the calves that were born regularly to our sixty or more milking cows and the two hundred beef cattle, even on occasion training them for riding. Cats were a neces-sity around the barn to keep the rat population down. Goats, especially kids, were just fun to have around. Dogs? Well, they were an expendable luxury.

Pet population control was part of farm life. At our age, we didn't know that birth control was even possible. The adults around certainly never talked about it, maybe because it was not affordable. The boys at The Home had grown accustomed to killing—one bump or dunk and the animal was gone.

Death had become a rite of passage for us. Maybe it was one way we could lessen our powerlessness at having been left at The Home, a world unto itself, apart from the one in which people knew that others loved them and knew whom they loved. Death, or loss, had visited most of us early in our lives, or else we would not have been there. Maybe we were just get-ting even. Maybe we were fighting shadows of our pasts. Almost all of us had killed pets before. Although we felt we had to do it, gradually we made the process more and more ritualistic, barbaric, detached. Death became a game, the source of a grim sort of pleasure.

Kittens would be held in a tub of water until they stopped breathing. I remember laughter. I wish I didn't. I wish I could wipe away the smirks that are still plastered on the faces of the boys in my mind. Some half-grown kittens, before they were dunked, would have their tails doused with lighter fluid and lit, just so we could see them scoot along the ground with their butts dragging to put the flames out. A couple were tossed from the hundred-foot-high water tower behind the dining hall, just to see if they could land on all fours alive. We seemed oblivious to our cruelty and to the torment it caused. Then there were the marches and the drums.

That summer morning we all finally understood how vicious we had been to have put away one loving pet after another. We killed something in ourselves each time. Lady taught us some-thing that we—the whole gang—still remember. Life is remark-able. Death is a passage and final. Time is short and fleeting. *Something*, I'm not sure what, is gone with the last breath. There is no going back, and there is no forgetting.

With the drumbeats filling the air, we all came running from various parts of the barn area to form our version of a brigade, lining up, two by two, stepping like the ill-prepared miniature military recruits with stick guns we used in games. We were big and proud. We began to march in place, shoe leather slapping the bare ground, but never in step with one another.

Most of us wore rolled-up jeans, stained and smelly from days of milking. Those who were wearing shirts had on the standard calico or all-white T-shirt, or Blue Bell denim. In those hot summer days in the South, we got two changes of clothes a week, one for work and one for after work. (Underwear? Well, you can imagine.) All of us had our brogans on, the earlier version of the type of work shoes that are now, much to our surprise, fashionable to our children. We hated them then, which is why we often chose to go barefoot—at least when we were not working and when there was no danger of having to walk through the waiting pens, where a kid could easily sink ankle-deep in cow dung every other step. We knew we couldn't avoid the dung on this trip; we were going straight through the sloppiest part of the holding pen.

Animal, a boy with short greasy hair and round-rimmed glasses, was the self-appointed executioner for most of these rites. His protruding muscles showed evidence of early puberty, but his empty smile revealed volumes about his simple mind. He took the role of lead sergeant, using his "bump-off stick" to direct us into a semblance of a marching unit. "All right, men, let's get this show going," he said as he moved along the lineup.

The bump-off stick, used solely for events like this, was Animal's pride and joy. I remember it as being six feet tall, but it was probably only three or four feet long, about two inches thick, made of solid oak, almost as hard and heavy as cast iron. It would have given any of us a headache with the slightest strike to the head. Animal had carved it himself, made it smooth to the touch, and personalized it with rounded grooves and his initials carved into the handle at one end. It also had a leather strap by which he swung it at the head of the march, the way a drum master swings a baton.

The notches on it told everyone just how much of a man

Animal was. He loved to show them off with a silly grin across his face. He had used the bump-off stick numerous times before that day, and each time the execution was swift and sure: one blow and the pet would be gone. Animal would immediately carve another notch.

"All right: everyone move out. Keep in line and in step. Don't mess with me," he said, as he popped someone on the back of the head with the palm of his hand for not paying attention. As usual, Mr. Panns, the pot-bellied, undereducated, sixtyish dairy boss, watched with approval as we marched by. *Rat-a-tat-tat, rat-a-tat-tat* went the drums. *Clunk, clunk, clunk* went our boots. Mr. Panns waved to us with one hand and with the other scratched his protruding belly, which stretched his shirt buttons to the limits. His jaw was also stretched to the limit with a wad of Red Man chew, but still he managed to watch us with a sneer and a grin. He knew exactly what we were up to. *Rat-a-tat-tat.*

Also as usual, a dozen of us boys marched two by two down the bare path that led around the milk room, through the holding pen, and past the feeding barn into the woods, just beyond the barbed-wire fencing on the other side of the trails that the cows used as they returned from the pastures. I seem to remember the drumbeats echoing back to us from the rolling hills in the distance.

Lady was pulled along, more like dragged, seemingly aware of where she was being led and what those drumbeats meant. We giggled nervously as we played this game of processional, adding our own "dum, dum-de-dum, dum, dum-de-dum," with an occasional blow on a make-believe bugle, as we went along and commenting on how "big" (meaning manly) all of this was.

Animal would pretend to correct us. We would pretend to follow his orders.

We climbed the fence to reach the thick grove of trees, some large and arching and some spindly, where the leaves were thick and spongy. We pushed the leaves aside to form the ceremonial circle, and Lady was tied to the thin maple tree in the center, as usual. Animal said a prayer with the usual smirk on his face, and blessed the dog who had been our loving pet but was now a measure of our virility. We all had our say. Someone pretended to sprinkle incense over Lady's head.

Animal smiled and raised his oak pole. The blow to the head was as crushing as an overdeveloped twelve-year-old boy could make it. He was proud of what he had done—a good lick, a sure lick, what should have been the last lick. We winced as Lady howled, bloodied and in pain, and drooped, but did not go down. Animal's leadership, his very manhood, was on the line. He had not felled the bitch in a single blow, which was his signature claim to fame. He made light, offered some excuse.

Angry, he raised the pole again, and again the blow was intended to be deadly, direct to the head. Lady's skull must have been shattered, but she did not fall, in spite of her trembling legs stretched out in front of her. She howled and looked directly at me, as if to ask, "Why? Why are you doing this to me? I love you. What have I done?" He swung again, again, and again. Still she did not drop. Again and again. Animal lost his composure. I rubbed blood from my shirt.

Lady dropped—finally—into the pool of blood that had drained from her nose. I turned away, hoping it would be over, but Animal kept swinging. He had to. Lady was down but she would not die, and there was no way to retrieve her from her half-dead state. Her howls kept coming, each weaker than the one before. Again and again, the club fell on her head, and we prayed that the ordeal would soon be over. We began to gasp. Someone yelled, "Stop! Please, *stop!*"

For a moment, after what seemed an endless beating, there was silence. Lady was silent. We were silent, stunned, shattered by the pain we had witnessed and Lady had endured, by the death that would not come. Each of us, with sweaty palms, cried silently in front of the others, feeling a new kind of pain mixed with relief that it was over. Animal hung his head, biting his lip and gripping his fist, glaring at the ground.

But it wasn't over. Just as we were accepting the end, Lady raised her head a little and let out a howl that pierced the woods—and my brain, indelibly etching that morning on my soul, and on the soul of every other boy there who mocked the living and the dead, and was in turn mocked by both.

Animal got the best of Lady before the morning was out, but he was sick to the gut. We were all sickened. We left the woods in silence. Those who had carried the crate tops dropped them there. Several of the boys went in different directions to walk alone in the woods. We all wanted to be alone. I went to hug my pet goat and sit in the corner of her stall in the back of the shed beside the hay barn. Dooley wandered to the top hayloft of the biggest barn, where he had made, by restacking the bales, secret passages to his own private "room." I don't know whether Animal ever notched his stick or even brought it back. I never saw it again.

At our lunch in Planesville decades later—the first time I had ever talked about that day—Dooley told me that he spent several hours in his makeshift room that day. After a time, I left the stall to walk with my goat. Dooley reminded me that a couple of the boys threw up when it was over. Animal ran away from The Home some time after the incident, as a few other children had done before. He faded into the world beyond the fence. All we ever heard about him was an unsubstantiated story that years later, with a cohort in his new life, he robbed his grandfather using the skills he had learned at the dairy. By then, Animal had supposedly graduated from clubs to guns.

Dooley and I remembered the events in the woods as though they had happened the day before. Yet, as with so much else that we had experienced, we had had to bury the pain and hostility inside. We had learned to pretend that nothing bad had happened. We were secret guardians of our internal tribulations.

In our need to place blame on someone who should have known better, neither of us has ever been able to forget the approving grin on Mr. Panns's face as we passed him on our marches. He would slap Animal on the back for getting rid of the barnyard problems. If only he or anyone at The Home who knew exactly what we were doing and how we were doing it, had told us not to march, not to play soldiers, not to mock the most abominable of all human acts, killing.

Dooley and I agreed at lunch that if Mr. Panns were still living and if we were ever to see him again, we would remind him of the experience we had that summer day at The Home, and of the torturous nightmares of Death on the prowl, of the howls that come from the grave of a dog, that we have had many nights since. We would tell him how ashamed we were then, and have been since, of what we had done. But then, Mr. Panns did not beat the drums or swing the stick. We had all had our share of private horrors, but they had been done to us. What was different about that ritual at the barns is that we made our own private horror, which is a category apart from the private horrors meted out by others.

After lunch, Dooley and I went back to The Home, a few miles from where Dooley now lives but a continent away for me, and returned to the spot deep in the woods behind the dairy barns, as we had done time and again in our minds. Mercifully, the place was not the same. The Home no longer exists as it was that summer. Its mission has changed. What was once an *orphanage* (how I hated that loaded, misunderstood word) is now a "crisis management center" for severely troubled children and their families. The cows were gone. The milking barn was gone, as were all but one of the dozen or so structures at the dairy. Even the fencing was gone. Lush fields of uncut grass grew where the waiting pens had been. The trees that had been twigs back then gave shade. The marking on a couple of slabs of wood we had left, "To Lady," had long since crumbled to dirt. We stood there in silence, hopeful that our being there would wear out the burden we had felt every day since. We got a bit of relief, but not much.

Dooley has become a lifelong member of his local humane society. I have no such formal commitments, but I continue to wince at the sight of an animal in pain. I still hear Lady's howls, but I'm glad I can hear them. CJ tells me he recalls that day but has no lasting problem with it—he still dunks the kittens he finds on his property.

The boys and girls from The Home are much older now, most gray or graying. We have made our way through the world, in spite of the odds people would have given us before going there. We found out something about ourselves along the way—about living and dying, good and bad, loving and leaving—but we never learned more in a passing morning than we did the day Lady died, when a measure of us died too. My only consoling thought is that a measure in each of us was also reborn.

When people learn that I grew up in a home for children, they invariably ask whether I was affected by it. Of course I was—to the core, but not always in the ways most people think. I am driven to create distance from my experiences at The Home and, at the same time, to return to them, to try to remake some of them and to relish in others. A friend reminded me of the second-century rabbinic phrase "my degradation is my exaltation." Those words must be puzzling to people who have never confronted penetrating personal trauma, the intense kind Dooley and I remember. They don't know the drive of making amends. They can't appreciate how degrading experiences can be inspirational, life-affirming in the end.

The Home is like a video in my mind, constantly being replayed in full detail. I still see some of the paths in the woods, the exact places where I climbed the fences, even the steps in the mud of the creeks, and I hear the sounds of the other kids as if I were still there. I remember my intense affection for the pets more than for the other kids—not that we didn't care for one another, or have fun, only that we seemed always to keep our distance from one another. We were good buddies, but we rarely connected at a deeper level, the way siblings connect in close-knit families. Maybe we were no longer able to connect, since our earliest connections had been severed. Maybe we were too caught up in coping. Those of us who went through The Home feel a warmth in being around others who made the same *trip* with us, but the warmth is more a consequence of the *place* we shared for a time than of those with whom we shared it.

Dooley, CJ, and all the other two hundred or so boys and girls will always be, in my mind, how they were back then, not what they came to be. I didn't take them along with me on the trip after The Home. I lost contact with them for many years as we each, having started at the same place and been touched by the same events, evolved into markedly different people.

But I do think about Lady a lot. And I often think about what life would have been like had I not gone to The Home, had I not been there when Animal vigorously swung his bump-off stick, had I not beat the drum that morning. My life since has been an attempt to rise above it all, to do a form of penance, to find the fortitude to make my way in an alien world that does not understand where I came from and doesn't really care, an attempt to beat the pack in spite of the fact that my gate didn't open with all the others.

For most children, home is just home, no capital letters, no "the" in front. We called home The Home as our way of noting every time we mentioned it that it was a place apart from the life outside its gates and the life we had known before going there. The Home is still called by its old name (in spite of having a radically different purpose), and the campus still straddles the same highway in North Carolina. A post office, which in the 1950s was hardly bigger than two phone booths, is still there. A few of the old buildings remain. But it was never so much a place as a way of growing up that is foreign to most children who grow up in the usual way (not in sleeping porches or cottages under the supervision of housemothers), who work little, and who have a tough time finding enough kids to play tag or pick-up ball games. The Home remains a state of mind and soul against which much of later life must be judged. The Home is something to be from. It is a standard to be above. It's where we all went for a chance to find a new life course. It sent us on our way, usually remade for the better.

In the 1950s, most of the girls and boys who lived there were not full orphans, meaning both parents were not dead. Many were half-orphans. Most were from broken homes. Few were illegitimate, as far as the children knew, and fewer still, if any, were severely disturbed children, the type you had to fear. Only one in my age group, Chandler, could claim, with the pretense of pride, to be "the only legitimate bastard" there. On Mother's Day and Father's Day, more than one of us would be the typical wiseass and wear a pink carnation (not the traditional red or white), pretending not to know whether one or the other parent was dead or alive.

But our fun with days set aside for honoring parents was nothing unusual. We always made light of family matters, to the extent that we knew our families, but then we made light of almost everything. No story was too lurid, no joke too untamed. None of us wanted to be tagged as an orphan, not so much because we didn't like the way we lived as because of the knee-jerk pity the O-word engendered in those who knew little of how we lived, who harbored only incomplete impressions of orphans from a century or more earlier. Nonetheless, like blacks who spurn the word *nigger* when used by nonblacks but jokingly use it among themselves, we at The Home spread the word *orphan* around among ourselves, usually in mock contempt, in such expressions as "you damn orphan!" And we did do some damnable things, as well as a lot of neat things.

Dooley and I walked back that afternoon from the spot in the woods toward where the dairy barn had been and our cars were parked. We didn't say much. We didn't have to. We didn't want to. We felt a bit more at ease.

In spite of all the ground that we tried to cover at lunch and on our walk into the woods, we still didn't know many of the details of each other's lives since leaving The Home. But we surely knew the forces that had worked on each of us and taken root on the ground we walked across. Few others we have met in our lives, not even our wives and children, have been able to understand those forces fully. It was good to spend an afternoon with someone who did.

Dooley got in his car and left. I told him I wanted to take one more walk to front campus. I didn't tell him that I wanted to walk to the spot—the very spot—where I had first set foot on the campus a third of a century before and set off on a course that took me to where I was that day. I wanted to relive the emotions of that scared little boy on that first day as his aunts drove off in a cloud of dust, as he toted his battered suitcase up the walk with strangers. I wanted to think about where I might be had I never gone to The Home. I wanted to find something of who I was in the details of the place where I parted company with a sordid past.

2

ARRIVAL

THE YEAR WAS 1952. THE RIDE FROM RALEIGH TO THE HOME in early September had been a long one for my brother, Wendell, who was then twelve, and me, ten. We sat quietly in the back of my aunt's 1942 Chrysler, listening as she and her sister chattered about how nice The Home would be for us.

The aunts were my mother's sisters. Neither one had graduated from high school. One had not completed elementary school. Times were tough when they had been growing up, forty or fifty years before. They both lived modestly but well in Raleigh. The older one, Aunt Bertha, was perpetually nervous, her voice always strained into a high pitch from tension. Her small brick house, which she shared with her mother, our grandmother, was always meticulously neat. But it was no fun inside for a kid; she had too many things that could break with the slightest bit of reckless behavior. In her house, I had to watch my every step, and I was never very good at doing that.

Aunt Bertha was a one-man woman. She had lost her husband early in the war and always talked about her Jim as if there had been no happiness since. She had become the family's matriarch, cold but giving. We had stayed with her and our grandmother, Big Mama, in the months before taking the trip to The Home.

Aunt Peggy was more animated, maybe because she was several years younger and had a child, so understood that children like my brother and me—especially me—could be imperfect, could even break a few things from time to time. She had married a barber twenty years her senior, who seemed always to be in a bad mood. Her marriage was not a good one.

Big Mama was different. She was big—barrel-shaped, her arms flapping with excess weight and her steely gray hair pulled tight in a bun on the back of her head—and the warmest person in the world. In fact, she was the only warm person in the family. What do I remember most about Big Mama? She hugged us. And she was always there. She was the person we went to after school until our mother got home from work. I never remember Big Mama going anywhere. She was just *there*—in the basement doing the laundry with the old-fashioned ringer tub, or out back by the clotheslines hanging sheets.

Big Mama made the best bread pudding in the whole world. I remember saving my pennies solely to buy a loaf of bread, so I could let it go a little stale just to have an excuse to ask Big Mama to make a pan of her pudding.

My brother and I were teary-eyed on the trip to The Home, terrified at our world being turned upside down, afraid of where we were going, not at all convinced that our aunts would be proved right about how nice it was there. Nice for them—sure. Not necessarily for us. The utter loneliness that would haunt me months later set in as I stared out the window, feet stretched forward touching the back of the seat in front of me, hands together between my knees, constantly twitching, looking side to side but seeing little.

Our aunts emphasized how many other children there would be to play with, how nice the grounds were. Years later I realized that they had never even seen the place and knew little about it—except that it was cheap. They told us that *they* would be making the payments. When I checked The Home's records decades later, I found that my father was supposed to be making the payments to my aunts, who would then pass them along to The Home. But he did not send the money regularly and eventually stopped it altogether, in spite of court orders.

I doubt that my aunts let my father know that they were taking us to The Home that day. I never heard him object. I didn't see him in the week or two before. On the way there, I must have wondered why he never came to say goodbye. We were on our way to spend the rest of our childhoods in an orphanage, and our father was back there, someplace, and I never knew where.

I experienced a complete feeling of emptiness—a total emotional vacuum—on that day as we made our way through Planesville, the last town before The Home. When we arrived at the edge of campus, school was in session. I didn't see any children on the grounds. My stomach knotted. My throat went dry.

The one great advantage—other kids—was nowhere in evidence. I felt betrayed. I knew I was being committed, put away, dumped.

The Home stretched for half a mile down either side of the highway, both sides completely bordered by chain-link fences. Concrete underpasses connected the east and west sides of the campus. The cottages, which is what they called the dozen or more two- and three-story brick living quarters, were on the west side of the highway, scattered through the groves of towering oak trees, whose leaves had begun to turn slightly with the slowly approaching Carolina fall. On the other side were the administrative offices, working buildings (carpentry shop, printing shop, boiler room, and canning shed), campus chapel, schools (Upper and Lower), farms, and railroad tracks.

That first day we were given a tour by Miss Winfield, a tiny, white-haired social worker with a perpetual smile. I remember the thick dust blowing up behind the car as we rode along the unpaved road that circled through the campus. No rain for days, we were told. It was hot and humid, a typical late-summer day in the South. "Look, that's where you will be staying, and your brother will be staying over there," she explained as she pointed out two different cottages. Kids were housed by age, not by family. Brothers and sisters, in particular, would wind up at polar ends of the campus because girls and boys had to be kept as far apart as possible. Siblings could visit in school and at meals, held in the main dining room, a large turn-of-the-century hall with a bell tower that was in the exact center of campus.

We said our goodbyes to our aunts, who left as quickly as they could. I stared at the car and the swirl of dust behind it.

But I didn't cry. I could not do that in front of people I didn't know. I kicked at a couple of rocks in the road until Aunt Bertha and Aunt Peggy drove out of sight.

Miss Winfield then took my brother and me to the elementary school, laughing and pointing things out along the way: "There's where you will be eating. Over there is where your laundry will be done. We have lots of animals on the farms, which are behind that row of buildings. We'll have a watermelon feast out under those oaks this Sunday. You'll love that. You can eat all the watermelon you want."

The school building for the first seven grades was old at the time, but typical of other country schools in the South. The auditorium, which doubled as the gymnasium, fully marked for basketball, was in the center of the building; the classrooms were around the sides. But the auditorium was dark, as so much else seemed in the building at the time.

Wendell went into the seventh grade, I into the fifth. I will never forget being led to the front of the class by Miss Kelley, the plump, buxom teacher. With both hands on my shoulders, she announced in an overly sweet voice to the class of twenty or so kids: "Look here, children, we have a new student. His name is Dickie." She paused to wipe her mouth (I came to learn that she slobbered all the time). Then, on some invisible but known sign, the children said in approximate unison, "Hello, Dickie." I was *in* The Home.

On the way there, our aunts had kept assuring my brother and me that we meant so much to them and explaining why they were sending us to The Home. They had to, they said. My mother had died four months earlier, two days shy of her thirty-ninth birthday and a week before Mother's Day. My father, eight years older than my mother, was a drunk, prone to fits of violence against my mother, which we had witnessed firsthand before their divorce when I was five.

I remember vividly watching in horror at the age of four as my father grabbed my mother by the wrist, throwing her out the front door and breaking her arm in the process. A small child does not forget seeing his mother in the dark of night sprawled on the front walk, sobbing in pain and frustration. It is hard to think that you are supposed to love the person who did it. Neither will I forget having to secretly unlock a bedroom door sometime after my father shoved my mother behind it. Even now I can feel the cold fear of cowering with my mother on the couch in the darkened living room, sobbing, pleading with my father to leave her alone, using my own body to shield her against any more strikes that might come.

I may have felt distressed at being in class the day I arrived at The Home, but I was not all that distressed at what I had left. One of the reasons I look back fondly at my life at The Home is shared by many other boys and girls who passed along its fences: it catapulted me from a life course that had no good end. I was given a chance to start anew. I didn't have to feign love and warmth anymore when there was none. I was part of a group of kids who would eventually become closer to me than my own brother. I faced a world of unexplored opportunities and, more important, strict limits and reasonable expectations. I could prove myself in a different way. I could give up the shadows I had been fighting.

I didn't want to have to fight anymore. I had found a place—

one with real, defined limits—at The Home, by no means a perfect place, but a place.

That September day in 1952 I wasn't taken in so much by The Home as by the twenty-five boys of Larr's Cottage, next to the vast playground (about the size of two or three football fields) on the south end of campus. All the boys at Larr's were in the fifth or sixth grade, which meant that most were ten and eleven (a couple were older, having been held back a year or two in school). Dooley was one of the smallest kids, but he was a good-looking child. When The Home needed publicity shots for its fund-raising efforts, he would always be dressed to look the part of an orphan worthy of supporting. Despite his poster-boy appearance, he could not resist engineering the clogging of the drains in the concrete underpasses before a major storm just to see how full they would get. With our help, he had them damn near overflowing on occasion.

Chandler, somewhat aloof and quieter than most, was clearly the brightest of the bunch, but that meant only that he read some in his spare time, not that he showed clear promise of being a scholar. He was vain as well, so obsessed with whitening his teeth that he had, by the age of twelve, bleached them gray, with a combination of baking soda and Ajax, in an effort to make them white. Wiley was chubby, and we teased him because his gut hung over his belt. He tried to act smart and serious, but he got little respect for his efforts. Mooney was our Alfalfa, snaggletoothed and freckle-faced, hair cut to the skin on the sides but slicked back on top, full of pompous oratory.

CJ was clearly the playful type, but a nonconformist to the core and incapable of taking anything seriously. Although he had a deep-seated fear of heights and closets, he was absolutely fearless in tackle football even at the age of ten, running with the ball straight through lines without pads or a helmet, with his head down. To the older boys, who could not believe his willingness to risk life and skull for an extra yard or two and who egged him on, he became known as "Rubberhead," a nickname that can cause him to recoil to this day.

CJ was also the type of kid who liked pets, the weirder the better. He found a mail-order firm that advertised raccoons for sale, $24 apiece. He never thought that it would take more than a first-class stamp to send the cash through the mail—in quarters and dimes. He got his two-pound package back, but never got the raccoon.

Bilton was about as mean and devious a kid as you would ever come across. He once got several of the boys at Larr's to put their Sunday bag lunches together for his planned attempt to run away. But instead of running away, he went to the woods to eat all the food. (He did carry through with his plans to run away, but years later.)

Animal was a boy who needed no finesse in dealing with the rest of us, and could not have shown any if he had tried. He had brawn that he used to good and bad effect, as you will recall from the last chapter.

Larr's was a cavernous building, very institutional-looking, so old its bricks would crumble at the touch. But it was clean, with wood floors shiny and yellowing from too many heavy coats of wax applied without precision by the children. There was little furniture in the big meeting room on the first floor aside from the dark-brown wood storage boxes, heavily scratched from much use, that lined the walls and a couple of institutional chairs and sofas, the kind with chrome bars on the ends and seats, covered with vinyl. A big light, with one of those cream-colored, faceless globes, hung in the middle of the ceiling of the large downstairs "playroom." Only a couple of curtains hung on what must have been ten-foot windows that surrounded the room. No lamps. No clutter. No real warmth, aside from the steam heat.

Sleeping? No private or semiprivate rooms in Larr's, to say the least. We had "sleeping porches" — rooms that extended from three sides of the second floor of the cottage, made of wood and windows, each lined with eight or more beds, each bed so tightly made that a quarter would bounce off. There was nothing else — no pillows, no bedspreads — only an old-fashioned quilt folded neatly at the foot of each bed.

If the concept of sleeping porches sounds bleak, or brings to mind haunting visions of a child's life with little comfort, you are probably thinking like a middle-class, middle-aged adult in the 1990s — not like the ten-year-old boy I was, thrilled at the prospect of having a slumber party every night for years.

Going to bed was fun, most of the time. Practically every night for the next two years, we would go to bed early — 8:30 was bedtime, no questions asked, no delays tolerated — and pretend to go to sleep. But as soon as the coast had been declared clear — that is, Miss Bauer, the housemother, went downstairs — we would break loose with jokes, farts, and giggles. Objects, from dirty underwear to an occasional water balloon, would sail through the air.

We didn't have pillows, but that didn't stop us from having

pillow fights; we filled cloth laundry bags with scrap cloth and other bags, usually when Miss Bauer had the night off and one of the "big boys" from the high school was in charge. We even plotted and carried out attacks on other porches, careful not to be heard by anyone. Water pistols were the ultimate bedtime weapon of choice. They could be used in all-out wars on other porches or just as a means of strategic attack: a quick squirt from a doorway, if sent with enough arch, could rain down on everyone after a retreat had been made. If water pistols were not available, we fashioned rough substitutes from plastic tubes and cloth plungers. Sleep rarely came early; it came most often only when everyone had had enough.

The sleeping porches were great—except in winter. They were unheated, and only a little heat would filter in to us from the upstairs corridors. But even that was not ours for long. The central steam-heating system was shut down each night at ten o'clock, and the boilers would not be fired up again until five the next morning. Getting to bed in the winter was always a rush, both in terms of the way we made it to our beds and in terms of the shock of cold against nearly bare bodies: we wore only our underwear. Pajamas would have added to the laundry, I suppose.

I remember standing at the door to the sleeping porch, swaying back and forth with my hands on the rim and counting "one, two, three, go!" On "go" I would run and jump under the covers, burying my head under the heap of country quilts. Then I'd breathe as fast as I could to warm up the sheets. On occasion, some jokester would make these winter jump starts all the more agonizing by deliberately leaving all the porch windows wide open.

Amenities were at a minimum, but they were never less than the minimum. We each had an open locker in which to put our few things. Each locker was about a foot wide and five feet tall, with one shelf at the top. They lined the walls of a separate upstairs room. You can imagine what a zoo it was when we were all trying to dress in the morning. The only chance at privacy I had was a little space in the hall for a used trunk my father had given me, but I don't remember taking anything personal with me, not even pictures of my family. There was no room for sentiment. We simply didn't dwell on the bad things that had happened to us before coming to The Home.

The bathroom was communal. Every night just before bedtime, we would line up against the wall at the far end of the upstairs hall outside the bathroom for the ritual of brushing teeth and going to the john, all under the watchful eyes of Miss Bauer. She would stand stoically, arms folded atop her protruding stomach, leaning against the edge of the bathroom doorway—more marshal than matron, more concerned with our getting the job done in an orderly way than with our hygiene. At times, she would let out a cry of "Ah, gee-hau-si-fats!" to add emphasis to her orders. Miss Bauer would pass out the toothpaste, keeping order and telling us when we were through. If a boy misbehaved, she wasn't above harsh words and a tough pull on the ear, at which point she would say something like, "Now, don't think you are the cock of the walk. Just don't try me. I'll show you," which could mean added chores or writing a thousand times, "I will not blow bubbles with my toothpaste."

Miss Bauer almost always had a stern frown on her face. You can imagine that with two dozen ten- and eleven-year-old boys, she had little time for smiles. But she was no ogre. Neal swears that once when he and Conner had sneaked off and Conner had broken several bones after falling from a tree, Miss Bauer waddled as fast as she could across the ball field to the woods, climbed the wooded slabs of the fence, and jumped down to the other side, landing on all fours in her hurry to help Conner. She never punished him for the offense. No one, as I remember, loved Miss Bauer in any motherly way, but we all knew we could count on her when the chips were down or some stunt went bad.

After supper and play every Wednesday and Saturday, we lined up in the hall at the top of the twisted stairs by the clothes closet, lit by a single bulb swinging from a cord; it was time for Miss Bauer to hand out our clean clothes. As we reached the doorway, we would call out our sizes — "medium," "large," or whatever — and Miss Bauer would pull from the stacks one of each: drawers, socks, pants, and shirt (normally, a striped T-shirt). No choice, and no complaining for fear of risking one of Miss Bauer's "gee-hau-si-fats!" Then we would dump the clothes in our lockers and scramble to line up again against the wall at the far end of the hall, towels around our waists, for our baths.

In the bathroom, everything came in threes: three toilets in a row, three sinks in a row, and three tubs in a row. We went in shifts, first to the toilets, then to the sinks to brush our teeth, and on to the tubs — three of us in each tub at a time. Thank God the tubs were oversized.

Nevertheless, we were a sight to behold: three deep in three tubs. Water didn't always stay in the tubs, and Miss Bauer had to break up more than one water fight. We always used to snicker when it was Animal's turn because his manhood showed every time he dropped his towel. He tried to sneak in to avoid the giggles. We watched Miss Bauer to see if she was looking. No one could tell.

The water was changed only every two or three shifts, which is why we scrambled to get to the head of the line (not that we wanted baths). Talk about rings around the tub. I didn't mind the dirty water nearly as much as I minded Miss Bauer at the door patrolling what we were doing—and watching as we jumped buck naked into the tub or whizzed away at the john. You gave up your modesty in a hurry at The Home. Jokes about "Little Dickie" started then, in the baths.

But all this was after I had gotten accustomed to the routines at The Home. Back on that first day, all I could think of was that I had been committed to an alien place, outside the mainstream of life and love, very much like an orphanage in Raleigh that I used to pass on my bike. I could see only the tops of the buildings at that orphanage above the hills that bordered the road I biked along. I knew that the kids in that home were to be pitied, if not feared. We had no idea what kind of kids they were, whether they were mean or just poor. Like many children growing up in the 1940s and 1950s, I was often told, "If you don't behave, I'll send you to the orphanage. See how you like it there." When those words came true for me, I began to see what went on behind the fence.

By the end of that first class day at The Home, my nails were bitten down to their nubs. I feared the other children. I didn't understand how I was supposed to deal with them, or they with me.

After class, Conner, an exceptionally serious but strapping

eleven-year-old (he had repeated one year of school) who had been at The Home for seven years along with his brother, Wiley, pulled me aside from the monkey bars. The other kids were going through one contortion or another on the bars, each trying to amaze the others with his agility, if not his foolishness. Several others were in the adjoining field trying to organize a kickball game.

Conner had taken it upon himself to be my mentor in the ways of The Home. He told me about his first day there. Even though he had been only four, he remembered clearly the feelings of emptiness and assured me that I would get over them. He told me how he was brought to The Home without any of his folks ever telling him where he was going. After being examined in the infirmary, he heard a noise and when he looked up, he saw his folks getting back in their cars, "without ever saying 'bye."

"After a while," he said, "you won't think much about your family. They'll probably forget about you, too. My folks never write, except maybe at Christmas. I don't even spend vacation with them." I don't know where he got the wisdom to remind me that I would never forget the bad stuff that had happened to me, but he added: "There's no point in talking about the bad stuff *here*. Everybody has had bad stuff happen. No point in competing. There's always someone around who has had worse stuff happen. Me, I could make your ears stand on end."

In those first few hours Conner told me about the rules, the written and unwritten ones, especially the one about not "running off," or going places we were not supposed to go, which was practically anywhere that Miss Bauer could not see from the first-story balcony of Larr's. Punishment was sure and swift: cleaning the toilets, losing privileges, or being assigned time in the Chair, the straight-back one at the darkest end of the downstairs hall. There was always the haunting threat that truly difficult kids would be sent to Jackson Training School, a juvenile detention center. What constituted "difficult" was left conveniently uncertain. We knew, however, that Jackson was no place we wanted to go. At least at The Home we weren't put in cells with bars on the windows. And, Conner pointed out, it was difficult for anyone to keep track of all the kids at The Home, which gave us a great deal of freedom. He probably didn't realize that he was dealing with a past master at breaking the rules.

So, of course, on my very first day, I "ran off" to the pecan orchards with Conner. He showed me how to sneak from tree to tree on the edge of the road to get beyond the ball field and the Quads, a group of four cottages in a square for older kids, to the woods and the small pecan orchard (which was no more than a couple of dozen trees that lined the dirt road to the peach orchards). We moved stealthily, sliding from tree to tree like characters in a B western.

I did two things that first day that I wasn't supposed to do— I sneaked off *and* I raided the pecan trees—but by doing so, I learned I was in a far different place than I had ever been. There were boundaries here. And, while they could be breached, they had to be taken seriously. I learned the joy of sharing a productive adventure with another kid, and he would be only one of many. There would be other days, other kids, other adventures. The past could be lost in adventures. The past could not get at me. The boundaries of The Home were also boundaries against my father, who, up to that day, might have gotten hold of my brother and me. I went through a tunnel that day. It was dark at the start, but I could see the light of a different future with the adventure.

Conner and I filled to overflowing a couple of small bags and the bottoms of our folded-up T-shirts with the best pecans I'd ever eaten. We had intended to sneak them back to Larr's and pass them out to the other boys when the lights were out. Our problem: getting past the house of The Home's director, Mr. Shanes, a stately, religious man with silvery temples and glasses the size of two quarters on gold rims. Mr. Shanes *knew* there was a right way and a wrong way to do everything. He *knew* heaven and hell existed. He knew God firsthand, I soon became convinced. He insisted, emphasized by deep, long, sucked-in breaths, that everyone toe every line because it was the godly thing to do. We feared him. Unlike his predecessor, who was dearly loved by everyone, Mr. Shanes was willing to send kids away for misdeeds. But during the years we spent with him, many of us came to respect him. He became a standard by which we, eventually, would judge our every move.

Conner and I made our way along the back line of Mr. Shanes's yard, confident that he was still at the office. Unfortunately, Mrs. Shanes wasn't. At the worst possible time, she came out her back door. We wanted to crawl into the brier bushes that prevented a speedy change in course, but we had nowhere to go. "Hello, boys, what are you doing? Where are you going?" she asked nicely, not for information, not for incrimination. She seemed not to have the slightest idea that we had done anything wrong, despite the obvious bulges in our T-shirts.

When Conner told her I was the new kid on the block, her eyes lit up. She made me feel I was where I should have been all along, there at The Home. She wanted me there, was glad to have me. She told me so. But then she asked what we had in our bags. "Oh, nothing, just a few pecans." A few? We had enough to feed the whole cottage, but we hoped those words would be the last on the subject. They weren't, and we were terrified when she offered to make us a pie out of them, something she said we could share with the other boys.

"Gee whiz!" was about the only response we could muster. On my first day, I had been caught red-handed with stolen pecans, and now the wife of the director was going to make us a pie. Conner and I knew we'd been had. We both choked and almost broke into outright laughter as we glanced at each other. Miss Bauer would be mad. Punishment was certain. Mr. Shanes would be enraged, and we—especially Conner—knew we would have to sit in the Chair for hours, mop the halls for weeks, maybe even go without food for a few days. We were goners. *And on my first day!* All we could do as we continued sneaking back to Larr's after we left our stash of nuts with Mrs. Shanes was gag and fret over the fix we had gotten ourselves into.

It wasn't over yet. We had to go get the pie. How would we explain showing up at our cottage with a pecan pie? We hoped Mrs. Shanes would forget about the whole thing.

But somehow she got a message to us the next day that the pie was done. We sneaked over, as we had to do. She wouldn't let us leave without a taste. We sat in her kitchen gulping what seemed to us the most illegal pie in the universe. We wanted to get out of there. She never let on that she knew anything was wrong, if she did. Even Mr. Shanes came in and had a piece with us without reprimanding us. Miss Bauer never said a word.

I smiled my way to sleep that night. I understood that there were problems in my past that could possibly, just possibly, be kept at bay. Those problems would become part of one of those momentous life puzzles that could not be assembled for years to come.

3

LIFE'S PUZZLES

My brother and I had been out playing tag that May day in 1952 at our Aunt Bertha's house. We understood that our game might be interrupted at any time.

Just before noon, Uncle Stephen, our mother's brother, called us in and, with his hands on our shoulders, led us into the small den at the back of my aunt's house. Wendell and I knew what he was going to say. We knew before he knew. Nevertheless, he proceeded slowly and somberly, measuring his words as he told us that Mother had died. I pretended to cry.

We had awakened later than usual that Monday morning. We smelled something. Both of us bolted upright in the double bed we shared in the apartment on Wilson Street. My brother, twelve, two years older than I, sniffed and looked worried. So did I. We rushed out into the living room to call for our mother, who slept on a foldout couch on the other side of our closed bedroom door. The room was saturated with gas fumes. In the kitchen, the oven door was wide open but no flame had been lit.

We knew the gas was deadly, the reason why my brother and I were not allowed to start the oven ourselves. It was the only part of the stove that didn't have a pilot light. Our mother was face down on the floor of the kitchen in her bathrobe, her feet straddling the kitchen entrance and her head maybe five feet from the oven door.

Holding our breath as tightly as we could, we struggled to drag her out of the kitchen and in front of the two living-room windows. They were not easy to open, even with both of us pulling, but finally we managed, gasping for air as each window gave way and yelling for help when we could. No one heard us. It was only then that my brother thought to dash into the kitchen to turn the oven off.

Daring not to pass through the kitchen, I ran out the front door and down the stairs of the small building, out the front door, around the building, and up the back stairs to open our back door. It was locked. My brother came through the kitchen to unlock the back door and let me in to raise the kitchen window. But, fearing the gas, I wouldn't go through. I retraced my path around the building and up the stairs.

While he fanned the air through the windows with magazines as fast as he could, I phoned Aunt Peggy, who lived ten blocks away. "Something is wrong with our mother. The gas was on. You've got to come." My aunt called the police.

Wendell and I turned our mother over, tapped her repeatedly on the face, shook her, asked her to wake up, pushed on her cheeks. Her skin was flattened against her cheekbone where it had been in contact with the kitchen floor. It was a little bluish, with a rubbery feel to it unlike anything I had ever touched. We took turns poking our heads out the living-room window for air and pleading with our mother to awaken.

My heart was racing so fast and hard I could feel it in my neck, then as now. The sweat on my palms was thick. I had never experienced death before, except in the movies, and I never wanted to think of what the stillness meant. Whimpers and odd sounds of terror punctuated the continuous babbling between my brother and me. "Come on, Dickie, pull. Pull. Can't you pull?" Wendell said at the same time he asked me to open the door to the apartment or to get a wet towel to dampen her face and neck. "I'm pulling as hard as I can. Is she dead? Wake up, wake up, please move, please don't die," I must have repeated a dozen times. My brother pressed me not to panic.

We stayed with her until the policemen and firemen came down the street, sirens blaring, after an eternity of minutes. They came through our open front door with masks on. A crowd of neighbors, including our schoolmates, began to gather outside.

The police found a neighbor down the street who agreed to take us in until our aunts could arrive. The lady made us a full breakfast—eggs, bacon, toast, milk, and anything else we wanted—and tried to make light of what had happened. "Oh, your mother will be all right. Everything will be okay," she yakked away. We knew better, but maybe there was some ray of hope. Maybe she had fallen ill. Maybe she was just out cold. We understood, down deep, that there was no point to the maybes. The hole in my world that had formed early in my life began to lose its bottom.

Sarah Bowman McKenzie had died by her own hand, the paper would later say. They — the detectives — came to that conclusion for obvious reasons: our bedroom door had been closed, not open as usual, and a towel had been stuffed beneath the door. Our bedroom window was open. All the other windows in the house were closed. She had been depressed (as all members of the family reported). Our father, who had by then been divorced from our mother for five years, never agreed. She was too fun-loving, too concerned about us, he thought.

I was able to play later that morning partly because I needed a diversion and partly because I didn't want to join the family in moping. Wendell and I were emotionally exhausted and wanted nothing more than to pretend that what had happened had not.

Still, for reasons I could not then have articulated, I also felt somewhat relieved that my mother had died, which partially explains why I pretended to cry when given the final word. I was afraid that a secret — my secret — would get out.

Most children have many photographs of their mothers. I have only two very small ones in which the features of her face are not clear. They show a woman with high cheekbones and a big but tentative smile. In an odd way, I prefer that the details of her looks remain obscured by time and the fuzziness in the pictures. I want to think she was a beautiful lady, as pretty as my daughter. I want to see my mother's eyes in my daughter's.

I have few good memories of my mother, although I know that early in my life she tried to be a good mother. She protected us from our father. She forged an escape for the three of us, risking the unknown consequences of his temper. I can remember the comfort she tried to give me at a birthday party when I could not sink my teeth into an apple in a bobbing contest. When I would start my nightly ritual of incessantly rocking, rolling from side to side in a chair, she would sometimes squeeze into the chair with me to hold me steady. I remember the comfort her hugs gave. She despaired when the school principal would call to say, again and again, that I had been in a fight on the playground. She left me with a few wise thoughts, like "don't brag; let others do it for you."

After my mother's death, the family members' biggest concerns, paradoxically, were to win the continuing, petty, post-divorce struggle with my father over control of Wendell and me and to remove us from their sight (and guilt). Aunt Bertha insisted that she was too nervous to handle us. Aunt Peggy tried to explain that she did not have room in her small house. Our uncle knew I would be a problem. My mother's third sister had the excuse of living in another state. They all wanted to rid themselves of the vestiges of a family embarrassment. Now, I can see that all their talk of concern for us was cheap, and fleeting. They simply did not want us.

Of course, after going to The Home, we got the usual cards and gifts from them for Christmas and birthdays, and we went back to Raleigh on occasion for short stays during "vacation" from The Home in midsummer; but over time the contacts became less frequent, the gifts less expensive, and the love less apparent. Within a couple of years, Big Mama died, and no one from the family ever came to see us at The Home. Eventually, my brother and I opted to stay on campus during our two-week summer vacations. We could dispense with all the pretenses, although the thought that we were not wanted was still a difficult one.

The aunts, before my father knew what was happening, had gotten custody of us—and with it, the right to put us in this Presbyterian orphanage. We—my mother, brother, and I—had not really followed any religion. I remember going occasionally to some Christian church in Raleigh (where I had been dunked in the pool at the front of the vestibule at too early an age), but I was never sure whether *Christian* was a designation for a denomination or just some word all churches used in their names.

The local Presbyterian minister, however, had "gotten us in" to The Home by pulling a few loose denominational strings and by claiming that we had attended his church (a lie he must have prayed to be forgiven for).

On reflection, I can't blame my mother's family all that much. My brother studied hard and did well in school—he seemed to be part of the flow of the world—but I was the child teachers didn't want in their classrooms: bratty, recalcitrant, prone to fights. I had become a child of the streets.

In my first ten years, we lived all over Raleigh. Our small apartments always seemed to be near some big landmark: the state university, the insane asylum, the capitol building on the square in the center of town. We were near the capitol when I started kindergarten in a Catholic parish, which was, I suspect, more a form of day care than a means to an education. Even those early years were a time of rebellion and petty crime for me. What I hated most about kindergarten was the morning worship before school. I will never forget how hard those kneeling benches felt against my five-year-old knees.

Because my mother had to be at work early, my brother and I walked the ten or so blocks to school by ourselves (even across busy intersections) most mornings. A schoolmate and I soon discovered with glee, however, that we could choose simply not to go in. We actually played hooky from kindergarten!

In class, I remember only two things. The first is that the nuns often asked us how many of us wanted to be priests and nuns. I always shot my hand up into the air, giggling at how easy it was to play their games. The second is the discovery that you could get the things you wanted just by taking them. The poor little girl with black curls who sat next to me, whose desk squared with mine, always left her lunch money in the book space under the top. Many a time I just reached over and eased the change to my side. I never got caught. I bought toys and bubble gum with the money.

I guess it was partly because I was such a problem that my mother had what the family called a nervous breakdown. Wendell and I were then sent off to a military academy for the second half of my first grade. There I constantly got into trouble for not obeying the rules, running my mouth, fighting, and refusing to eat the boiled okra that seemed to be a favorite of the cooks. The woman at the head of our table forced me to eat it, and all I could do was gag. To this day, I hate the sight of okra. I can't so much as smell it without feeling sick.

The housemother did something much worse to me than that. I was a bed wetter without equal. At age six, I still wet the bed just about every time I got in it. The academy punished me for it, time and time again, including having me do laps around the concrete circle in front of the dormitory. Come to think of it, I did laps all the time for everything.

I usually tried to stay awake during the afternoon naptime. I never wanted to sleep then anyway, but I was also avoiding the opportunity to do the dirty deed. The last straw with the academy was when I made the mistake of falling asleep one afternoon and, naturally, wetting the bed. The bitch of a housemother had had it with me. She tied my dripping sheet around my neck to wear for the rest of the day. A lot of people have done hurtful things to me in my life, but I have never been able to figure out how someone whose job it was to work with kids could have been so abusive. I can still hear the laughter and scorn of the other boys as I walked to dinner that evening with the sheet still in place.

When my mother recovered from her immediate problems with nerves, my brother and I went back to Raleigh. I went back to running the streets, playing hooky, getting into fights, shoplifting—and perfecting my yo-yo skills. Yo-yoing was about the only thing I did well, and I won a lot of yo-yo contests. But I had trouble passing every grade. My teachers, nonetheless, advanced me, supposedly for "social reasons." The most likely reason is that they wanted to pass along their problem kid.

By the time I was eight, I had crisscrossed the city on my bike. I had also been hit by a car. I was in a bike race with another street-running friend around our block, which was then up the street from the asylum (where all kinds of crazy people lived, so we were told). I wasn't going to let a simple little stop-light prevent me from besting my friend—or risking being bested by him. I was also confident that I could beat the car that was pulling away from the light to my left; I knew I could take the driver in the straightaway, if I could just make it to the straightaway. Barring that, he would certainly see me in time to avoid hitting me. But he didn't notice me.

The car literally ran over me, leaving tire prints on my thighs just above the knees but no broken bones, only a lot of abrasions and fluid in my left knee, causing it to swell and lock up. Fortunately, the car was a smallish 1942 Ford, about the size of a Volkswagen bug. When the driver stopped, my head was a foot from the back tire. Remarkably, the driver and my mother, who was hysterical but probably not surprised, thought nothing of pulling me out from underneath the car, propping me up in the front seat, and speeding off to the hospital five or ten miles away without calling for help.

My great fortune that day, aside from not having been killed, was one that I now regret. The driver of the car that hit me and took me to the hospital was black. In those days in Raleigh, a black man had little chance of explaining to a court how he could not have been at fault in running over a white boy. He was also apparently guilt-ridden and I did nothing to assuage his guilt, although I knew the accident had been my fault. His insurance paid all of the bills, with a little left over for me to squander years later when I turned twenty-one.

If it had not been for the accident, however, I might never have passed third grade that year. My third-grade teacher decided to give me school credit of a sort for the accident, to make up for the eight weeks of school I had missed. She assumed that I would have made passing marks if I had been able to attend. Like my other teachers, she found a convenient reason to pass me on.

The rest of my first four years in school can only be described as problematic, both inside and outside the classroom. I just could never learn to spell all those words, no matter how hard I tried. Worse, I shoplifted, took money from my mother's wallet, sassed, wrote on walls (at a time when few others did), and continued to play hooky. A school chum and I skipped school one winter day and nearly burned down a vacant wooded lot trying to stay warm by starting a fire. No one could see us from the road or from the nearby mom-and-pop grocery stores. The breeze was brisk and cold, and we used up nearly a box of wooden matches trying to get the fire going. We also used an inordinate amount of paper, which, just as the fire started, blew into the nearby dry grasses and bushes. We high-tailed it, but luckily someone managed to put the fire out before the firemen arrived. We never got caught, but I don't believe my mother was ever convinced that I had nothing to do with it once she learned I was not in school that day.

By the end of third grade, I had broken into my elementary school at least three times (for what purpose I do not remember), and I was regularly sneaking into movie theaters without paying. If the back door was locked, my friends and I would pool our funds to cover the admission price for one of us, who would, during a dark scene, open the rear door. The bad guys in the B westerns had nothing on us.

In those early years, I made money in a variety of ways, almost always without permission. When I was supposed to be at the local Y after school, I polished shoes on the main street in downtown Raleigh. I also sold newspapers. The business was supposed to be divided, one streetcorner per paper boy, but I found that my cherubic seven-year-old face could sell more papers simply by invading the businesses on the bigger boys' blocks—a practice I soon dropped after being roughed up by the older kids who enforced the territories. I took up other lines of work.

A friend and I made money by collecting coat hangers and selling them to cleaners, but not always on the up and up. We would ask for hangers at people's front doors, but we didn't let unlocked garage doors stop us from searching when no one answered the front door. We also made money by selling reclaimed golf balls found in ponds on the course near my aunt's house, but we didn't always look for errant balls. On occasion, we hid out far from the tees until golfers hit their balls near us, only to run out onto the fairway to retrieve them and then dash off into the woods, as the golfers yelled like hell after us.

Later life is, in a way, a process of putting together again the pieces of a puzzle of one's most dramatic and confused past experiences. It has been for me. The pieces of the puzzle of my mother's death and my relieved reaction were thrown about and then hidden in the dark corners of my mind, where they might be forgotten forever. The problem child I must have been for my mother formed pieces that were quickly put together, but there were other pieces that took years to assemble.

Child-care professionals understandably recoil at the thought of pulling a child from a loving mother or father and sticking him or her in an institution of any kind, but their mistake is in forgetting that, for many, the bond has already been radically severed, or needs to be.

My mother was a serious alcoholic, an "everydayer," as was my father, whom our aunts had blamed for my mother's alcoholism. According to my aunts, my mother started drinking with my father to keep him home. I vividly remember searching for the liquor bottles and emptying them down the toilet, leaving less than a jigger's worth in the bottom. Everyone knows what urine looks like in a toilet. Only a few children learn the color of bourbon mixed with pee.

My mother was always angry when she discovered that I had emptied her last bottle. Once she accidentally gashed me in the eye with the long metal vacuum-cleaner rod while trying to force me out from underneath the bed, where I had hidden when she came after me. We told the cab driver who took us to the hospital and the doctors in the emergency room that I had fallen on the rod. It has faded over the years, but the scar is still there in the corner, where my nose meets my eyebrow. The scars inside have never faded.

I have few memories of my mother sober during the last years of her life. I even more rarely remember my father sober, before or after her death. That isn't to say both parents weren't sober more than I give them credit for. It's just that my good memories of their days of sobriety don't jump ahead of all the bad ones.

Two days before my mother died, we had been over at Aunt Peggy's. Our aunt didn't drink, but my mother went prepared. She drank herself into another stupor, and when we walked back to our place, she could only stagger along. My brother and I ran ahead, staying close enough to help her up if she fell but far enough away that the distance might lead passersby to think she was not *our* mother. When she died, I was relieved partly because there would be no more embarrassing moments like that night.

My mother's drinking had taken her to the point of embarrassment and ridicule by her children, and maybe further, to levels of depression and self-abuse that I cannot imagine. She coped, she had to, but not always as I would like to remember. Our father rarely, if ever, contributed to our support. Her typing job with the North Carolina Department of Labor did not pay enough for us to have a car or to rent an apartment with a second bedroom. She had to sleep on the pull-out couch. I was a constant problem at school and everywhere else. And then there were the men, pieces of a puzzle that I could not understand until much later in life. I suppose I didn't want to understand.

Back then, all I understood was that the men, the ones we would meet in a beer joint we frequented, came to our apartment, often several at a time. Sometimes, they played with me. They didn't stay long, and I never knew where my mother would go when one was playing with me.

Another big piece of the puzzle remained missing for even longer. I knew at the time of my mother's death, without consciously acknowledging anything, that I had something to do with it. I didn't turn the oven on, but I might as well have. The relief I felt when she died was because of what had happened the day before. She was drunk that Sunday morning, as she seemed to be on all Sunday mornings, and I dared to ask her to let me do what the men had done. What happened in the next few minutes has haunted me, consciously and unconsciously, ever since. I understood what was being breached as I touched her, in spite of my curiosity and giggles. I suppose she did, too, in spite of her stupor and her inexplicably allowing me to do it.

Sometimes I think she put an end to her life so she would not have to look me in the eye after that day. She knew she had sunk as low as a mother could sink. She knew that I would be relieved. That was the really big piece of the puzzle. Our little secret went with her.

I gained a new lease on life the day my mother died. When, decades later, I finally came to terms with my role in her death, I felt like saying, "Mother, it's okay. I'm all right. You did the best you could for me."

In the spring of 1952, at the age of ten, I became a natural economist. I knew nothing as a child, of course, about arcane theories of markets. I did, however, come to see the world at the age of ten from a detached perspective—as an analyst/observer apart from the flow of events—as a place full of imperfections and limitations, where time is the ultimate constraint. I began to see everyone as imperfect, to one degree or another. I also began to see the inevitability of tradeoffs in an imperfect world and the need for forgetting, to the extent possible, about costs that can't be recovered. I realized I had to make adjustments on the margins of life, given the hand I had been dealt. Economics came naturally to me because it starts with the presumption of boundless imperfections and works through the need to be alert to hidden gains in needed adjustments on the margins of work and life. I was full of small imperfections and a couple of very big ones. I might be able to adjust upward.

People often wonder where some people get the drive they

have, and I have plenty of it to this day. I got part of the drive I have the day my mother died. I knew I had to rise above where I was, to do better than I had done, to be someone my mother could not be. I had to be someone in whom my children could see the kindness of my mother, to finish the type of person she possibly could have been. I knew someone would be watching. I had to fill the hole. My problem was I didn't know how to do it. The Home gave me the opportunity to make a break with my past, and maybe — just maybe — make amends.

The people who sent me to The Home could not have realized they were giving me a break with my past and a chance to forget, for a spell, how my mother had ended her life and the part I was convinced I played in her death. (I was able to pack that thought away in some recess of my mind.) The social-work fad today is to try to keep families together, even at high cost. The current government policy is to avoid institutionalizing children even when they have been neglected or abused at home, to support the faltering families with regular paychecks, to congregate them in rows of high-rises, to respect the rights of parents to keep their children no matter what. This policy unwittingly ensures that many children remain trapped, with deepening holes in their souls.

I've always had passions. I rarely do anything without a sense that the clock is ticking away, without a single-mindedness of purpose. Currently, two interests have converted themselves into something approximating passions. One is watching *Cops*, a television program that is, basically, a video record of police officers on their beats. And the other is using computers, like the one on which this book was written. While I understand little about how computers operate at the electronic and mechanical levels, I am greatly impressed with their capacities.

When *Cops* is on, the world in my house stops. I sit virtually motionless to watch it. I am often mesmerized by the episodes, constantly searching for meaning in the sordid tales that the ordinary cops on call frequently uncover; sometimes they can only shake their heads in horror when they arrive at their calls' destinations. Even seasoned, jaded cops can't comprehend how some people can live the way they do, do the things they do to themselves and each other, treat and mistreat their children the way they do.

I am especially hooked on the domestic violence calls, which usually involve some drunk or drugged-up mother or father — half-clothed, dirty, slobbering through the words of ill-conceived sentences — staggering about in the street after having knocked the hell out of the other. The house is usually filthy, sink filled with dishes, dog food (if not dog crap) scattered on the floor, trash everywhere, the smell of urine palpable even through the television screen.

The small children at the scene? They have witnessed it all, and too often are found curled in the corner of a couch, whimpering, or stumbling about a room not knowing which way to turn. Their stares are blank, their eyes glazed over. They seem to want to look nowhere, to hear nothing more, to find an escape where there is none.

When I see those children and reflect on my own life course, I can't help but think that the mind of a child is something like the hard drive of a computer. They can both be personalized and programmed. They can store one whale of a lot of information. All of life's experiences are stored in the hard drive of the mind. Like the hard drive of the computer, some experiences can be erased.

The mind and a computer's hard drive are unlike, however, in one important regard. With a computer, everything can be erased; all of the gigabytes can be wiped clean. In the case of the mind, on the other hand, some experiences remain, perhaps weakened, in spite of their being written over time and time again.

I have these thoughts whenever I look into the eyes of the children on *Cops*. Don't their parents understand that the children are recording everything, even when they appear detached—*especially when they appear detached*? Don't they realize that many of the recorded experiences will come back to haunt the children time and again in bits and pieces?

I am especially struck by the fact that for the children on *Cops*, there is no out, no escape—just a life with, in all probability, more of the same. The unstated tragedy of each domestic call is that the children are trapped by what has happened, fixed in place for their many young years.

I was a *Cops* child, so to speak, when there were no video cameras, no televisions, no VCRs present. If I were one today, I would not be given the escape that I was. I would not have the chance to reset my sails and my life course. The Home would not be there for me. I would have had to be far worse a little boy to be given an escape. My situation would have had to have been far more desperate. I would not be writing this today. I would not have been given the chance. Some agency would have tried to ensure that I remained in my father's or aunts' care. My father would have jumped at the chance to receive regular checks, but I would have then been on his path, starting where he was, trapped with what he would have provided.

People who observe homes for children from afar often assume that the children inside would all prefer to be adopted or in foster care. That is hardly the case. I don't ever remember a buddy at The Home lamenting that he wanted to return to where he came from, although a few did. Not all children liked The Home to the same degree, of course. Some ran away, but few of the runaways ran home.

Adoption was not an alternative for my friends and me. We could fantasize about the perfect loving home, but we knew that, *on average*, we were better off where we were. We saw things in terms of what we could *expect*, based on the probabilities, not the glorified exceptional cases.

In my first year at The Home, a rumor spread quickly that a nice young church-loving couple, interested in adopting a ten- to twelve-year-old child, would be walking the campus with the intent of picking one of us out. On the day they came, several of us headed for the woods; others eyed the couple from afar, securely hidden from view. None of us wanted to be adopted, to have to make another adjustment, to give up the security we had found, to take the risk of another shuttle to another place that might be worse. The Home was far from perfect, but it had one advantage: it was *there*, and we knew it would always be there. Foster-care kids understand that others hold practically all the cards and may use them without the children's interests in mind.

When I was in the tenth grade, Mr. Shanes called me into his office. I was concerned, but need not have been. Phillips Exeter Academy, the elite New England prep school, had offered The

Home a full scholarship for one of the boys. I wasn't a great student at the time, but I had changed immensely from my earlier years (for reasons that will become apparent) and was then one of the top two students among the boys. (Chandler was the other.)

I was distraught at the prospect of being selected, but I didn't know why. I was relieved when Chandler was picked instead. If it had been me, I might very well have gone further than I have. One thing is for sure: I would not have known why I went as far as I had. "Was it me? Or was it the academy?" would have been the questions that I could not, at this stage in my life, have answered with much clarity.

Children of The Home don't always envy the children whose spoons are silver. The children with silver spoons have one big *dis*advantage: they can never be sure whether they could have "made it" without that spoon. Their puzzles can never be finished.

Children of The Home know that if they fall from grace, they will be in familiar territory. They understand that they can do it all over again. They still have what they started with, a set of life experiences, and grit, that cannot be taken away. Those benefits and problems of growing up from the bottom became fully apparent to me in my first months at The Home.

4

FIRST CHRISTMAS

LIFE AT THE HOME THAT FIRST FALL HAD A RHYTHM AND ROUTINE that rarely varied. Get up early. Go to school. Go to lunch. Go back to school. Go to work. Go to supper. Play. Go to bed. At all times, follow the rules.

The Home needed the rhythm, I suppose, to maintain order among the two hundred children. We needed the rhythm, I suppose, to know where we should be and when. I know I needed it. My previous life had depended on what my mother had had to drink the night before, which usually gave me the liberty to do as I pleased. A mother in bed with a hangover can't exert much control over her children, or hold much of their respect.

Well, The Home surely changed all that, much to my liking, but it took me a while to see it that way. First I honed to a fine art bitching about the constraints imposed on me, a practice that led Miss Bauer to record in my file, "Dickie has had difficulty adjusting." A minor understatement.

Most people who did not grow up in a home for children judge it by what they see and don't see, what the children have and don't have. The children there have a different perspective, comparing what they have and where they *are* with what they had and where they *were*.

There were many school mornings that first fall when I would have preferred to stay in bed beyond 6 A.M. I would have preferred to have had a pillow to lay my head on. I would have preferred that the other boys be less rowdy in the morning. I would have preferred not to have to stand in line, dancing in place upon waking, waiting for the toilet. I would have liked for Miss Bauer to be kinder, to have more eggs and bacon and less cereal and toast for breakfast.

I would have preferred to have been able to walk to the big dining hall (which seated over three hundred) up the hill at my leisure, by myself—not with everyone else in Larr's—to join the other campus kids for breakfast. I would have then preferred more disorder at breakfast, not always having to stand quietly behind my ladder-back chair with six other new children at the special table in the center of the room. I never liked waiting to eat until the bell rang and the blessing was said. I didn't like being told how to behave, how to eat, when to talk, when not to talk. I wanted to be able to leave the table when I wanted, not always at the strike of the second bell exactly twenty minutes after the first one.

I was lucky that I didn't always get what I wanted. I got what few outside observers would know I needed: some restraint.

My first thought that fall was to rebel, to fight the restraints, as I always had. My better thought was that there would have been no point to it. The Home was too big. Miss Bauer, Miss Winfield, and Mr. Shanes were too serious — one big unflinching threat, presenting a united front. Punishment loomed certain and swift, and I was one of many to receive it. Although I did not stop rebelling altogether, I realized that it would mean devoting what little free time I had to the work of cleaning what had already been cleaned, as punishment.

Later in life I would write a book about being *bound* to be free, a treatise on the inextricable linkages between identified constitutional bounds on governmental processes and personal freedom. In one sense, the book had nothing to do with The Home. But in another sense, it was probably there that I had my first lesson on the necessity of boundaries in order to develop productively at the personal level. People who have been without bounds know what it means to be "bound to be free." Grudgingly and gradually, I discovered the value of boundaries. They don't restrict opportunities; they expand them, often by the day.

After breakfast we would race back to Larr's and finish our assigned chores — sweeping the porch, cleaning the toilets, mopping the halls, even sweeping (not just raking) the bare place under the monkey bars — in time to have a free moment to do what we wanted before school. That typically meant screwing around on the monkey bars, taking up a marathon game of Monopoly, or perfecting our shots in marbles. Then it was off to school by way of a walk across the middle of campus, under the north underpass, and then left down the path by Woman's Cottage (the dorm for the high school girls) to the Lower School (the Upper School was on the other end of campus). All with *no shoes!*

I'm sure that passersby driving along the highway that split the campus pitied the way we dressed: oversized jeans or shorts, calico T-shirts, bare feet. I thought going barefoot was the greatest invention of all time—but only after my feet toughened. We did not have to wear shoes in warmer weather, except for Sunday church and work, and we rarely wanted to.

Come late November, however, it can get pretty cold in North Carolina, making shoes a matter of necessity (and choice). Every year, the kids from each cottage would take their turn piling into The Home's green bus and heading for Belk's Department Store in downtown Planesville, barefoot but with socks in hand. Belk's could not compare with today's department stores. It was old even then, with creaking floors and no escalator or elevator, only stairs that squeaked louder than the floors. It covered three small floors, each hardly bigger than today's single-story drugstores, with a small adjacent store for the shoe department. Most of the clerks were grandmotherly and very southern.

I will never forget the day I got my first pair of shoes while at The Home. Our bus pulled up in front of the store and passersby watched us file inside. The front doors were locked because there was little room for anyone else once the boys of Larr's took over the store. The staff had been notified in advance and had hired extra clerks for the day. One clerk measured, another pulled a pair of shoes from a stack that had been readied for the occasion. There was no choice on the work shoes, only one brand and one style of heavy brogans with thick brown soles and toes that would not crush under the weight of a cow. "Size six and a half D—next," the clerk doing the measuring would say. For regular shoes, those we wore to school and church, three styles were pulled out, but they left little room for real choice; all three were low-cut, brown, thick-soled, and heavy. (A pair of sneakers could be come by only if you played sports or had them sent by family.)

The bus driver would try to keep order, but by the time we left, each clunking along in his new shoes, the shoe department was in chaos, with unboxed shoes and tissue paper everywhere. We were told that Belk's always gave The Home a special deal, as did many other firms in the area.

The exact size and style of those first shoes have long since faded from my memory, but the trip left a lasting impression for another reason: it was also the first time I realized that other people saw me as an orphan, as someone apart, different. None of us could ever get used to the tag *orphan*. It meant kids without shoes, without parents, without mouths wiped clean, without a lot of things. It meant pity, and we never wanted to play on pity. It meant the pitiful scene in the dreadful dungeon of an orphanage that Charles Dickens created in *Oliver Twist*, the one where Oliver, having drawn the wrong straw, must approach the cook and dare to utter weakly, "Please, sir, I want some more." We hated the misconceptions. We only wanted to make fun among ourselves of those who pitied us.

I tried, even at Belk's Department Store, to blend into the woodwork. Come to think of it, I've always tried to shirk off the label. Only in later years have I been able to admit freely to people that "I was an orphan," with the emphasis on the *was* and an immediate attempt to explain that it wasn't what they were thinking.

In the late 1950s, I saw the movie *I Passed for White*, the tragic story of a fair-skinned black woman who pretended, for a time, to be white. That movie struck a chord with the children at The Home because we all seemed to want to pass for something else when we were "off campus." On campus, no one thought you were anything different. No one pitied you. You would think that it would be easier for an orphan to hide his or her status in life than it is for a fair-skinned black to hide his or her race. But when we were off campus, or when donors came to The Home to see where their money was going, we were in constant fear that people could spot us from a mile off.

Life became a competition that first fall. We would race everywhere. Each of us would try to throw every ball the farthest, climb every tree the highest, spit the farthest (we called it "oyster throwing"), build the biggest fort, or explode with the loudest fart (the real kind or, in desperation, the kind made with your hand in your armpit). There was no way I could win fights (the other boys had been at The Home longer and were tougher than I, and there was a definite hierarchy reminiscent of life in the animal kingdom), and little chance I could win races on foot. But I just possibly could be the best in arithmetic. When Miss Kelley gave an in-class math assignment, I would rush to be the first to complete it and place it on her desk. Pretty soon we, girls and boys alike, made the run to her desk a race.

We were given workbooks in arithmetic that fall to finish in lockstep, month by month. Dooley, CJ, Chandler, and I would have nothing of that measured pace. We would meet in the cold far corner of an upstairs locker room after the lights were out at night, flashlights in hand and butts to the floor, to move ahead of the class. We had the workbook finished by the end of October. We may not have learned much — learning, as I remember it, was not the point — but *we had won!* The others were amazed. We beamed. I was shocked that I had taken something about school seriously, even if it was only to win another race.

Outside the classroom, work needed to be done. Cows needed to be milked. Crops needed to be grown and harvested. Meals needed to be cooked. Things needed to be fixed. The Home tried to feed itself — well, not totally, but as much as child labor, with the help of a few hired grownup hands, or "bosses," would allow. Even if work had not been required to put food on the table, Mr. Shanes would have required it. He thought that idle hands were the Devil's workshop. Work, in itself, he thought, was good. It turned boys and girls into men and women. On reflection, I think he was right.

The big boys did the heavy work in the fields and at the carpentry and print shops. The big girls did what was considered (inside and outside The Home) women's work: laundry, sewing, cooking (aside from breakfast in the fall and winter, when the older boys who played football and basketball took over). Older girls were also assigned to be aides to the housemothers of the smaller children. Those of us in Larr's were ten or eleven, but we still picked apples from the time we could get to the orchards by tractor and flatbed trailer after school until 5:30 or so each weekday and then again on Saturday mornings. Before work on Saturday mornings, we first had to change our bed linen, with the one clean sheet we would each be given. The top sheet from the previous week went on the bottom, the new sheet on the top. Even making beds became a contest over whose bed was the tightest and most wrinkle-free.

You can imagine that all these contests did not leave the cottage without strife. Losing was particularly difficult for Digger, who fancied himself one of the strongest in the cottage, although he was one of the smallest. By all accounts, he was a mean little son of a bitch, ready to put up his dukes or jump anyone who might cross him or mess him up at bed-making time. Regardless of how many fights — and they were few and far between, and nearly all kept from the attention of the housemother — by 8:00 A.M. on Saturdays, we were back working together in the orchards, in the potato fields, or in a brigade sweeping across the campus to clear it of trash. Saturday afternoons were our own, to do with as we pleased, more or less. Sundays belonged to God.

The apple-picking job seemed endless, given the vast acreage of apple trees. We picked and we picked, on the ground with buckets, up in the trees with large canvas bags around our necks (the kind with trapdoors on the bottom for easy emptying). To the trailer to empty, then back to the trees.

The sweat and boredom of the chore were broken only when the boss would go off. Then we would suddenly be at war. Apples are perfect missiles. Being hit by a hard ripe apple doesn't feel too great, as I can fully attest. On the other hand, it is exhilarating to hit someone else, especially with an apple at either extreme: green or well past rotten. We looked for the rotten ones, making piles of them as we picked out the good apples, just in case a war might erupt without warning.

I suppose most ten-year-old boys think of "pecks" as something birds do. We thought of them as buckets, four buckets to a crate. Crates were stacked at least six or seven high on the trailer, just high enough not to topple over as the trailer would sway from side to side on its way along the rutted field roads back to the apple barn, the cold storage room, and the cider presses.

Before that fall, I had been a scrawny kid. After hoisting crates that seemed as heavy as I was, I thickened. You could tell boys from The Home more by the veins in their arms than the shirts on their backs.

Play followed work, as well as broke it up. Getting together a game of kickball or softball or any other kind of ball was never a problem. During our free time, the large field outside Larr's was always teeming with kids wanting to do something, to drain their last bit of energy before and after supper (we never went to "dinner"). We looked to the older boys to show us the finer points of throwing a football or catching a "long bomb" on the run.

Basketball was immediately my favorite. Most days I could practice on a dirt court beside one of the cottages. But there was also a relatively new gym next to the farm that was fully marked for basketball (and doubled as a skating rink). That fall I could barely get the ball to the basket from the foul line, but within a couple of years my range had been greatly extended, more attributable to hoisting apple crates and hay bales than to court practice.

The Home had its own high school teams in football and basketball. While we were never a very big school, we always performed well in competition in those days. I suppose all the work we did made us stronger than our rivals, and it was so easy to put together a pickup game that we got in a lot of practice over the years. Football practice began at age seven or eight with the "midget league." The little tykes would play their hearts out in full gear. The older boys did most of the coaching.

Years later, when I was in the tenth grade, the supply of children at The Home had dwindled with the war and the rise of the foster-home system. There were only twenty-seven boys at The Home then eligible to play varsity football, and I was one of them—a strapping 131-pounder. Nevertheless, I made first team guard—*on offense and defense* (much to my regret)! I wasn't all that good. I made first team for only one reason: my "sub" was 116 pounds—soaking wet. The backfield that year had an average weight of 149 pounds, 7 pounds heavier than the front line. The quarterback, believe it or not, was the heaviest person on the team at 172 pounds.

As lean and mean as I may have been after years of farm work, I wasn't anywhere near as tough as I should have been for football. Everyone I played against that year weighed at least 75 pounds more than I, and I once played against an all-state guard who more than doubled my weight. Coach Stiger insisted that the experience would make me tough. I looked at it as getting the hell beaten out of me.

I stayed with football that first year and the following years, but not for any need to prove my toughness. I continued because it was expected of me. We won four of the seven conference games we played that year against schools some ungodly multiple of our size, and we gave the conference champion a real run for the game ball.

I remember getting hit so hard on one play that for a stretch of time I could remember little more than that I was on the field in a game. At The Home, you never, ever asked to be taken out of a game. You just faked it. Conner collapsed after playing without relief for almost the entire game on offense and defense in ninety-five-degree heat and humidity. I still don't like football. But I do like the memory of our team playing well, in spite of the odds.

But winning was not everything. Fair play was. Good sportsmanship was demanded. The surest way for a player to be pulled from a game and be sent packing to the locker room was to get in a fight on the field. The surest way for a boy or girl in the stands to be sent away from the game and to their rooms was to be caught booing. One of the grand traditions at The Home was to invite the opposing teams who played on our field to supper (games were always played in the afternoons; there were no lights on the field). The members of the opposing teams would be held back from entering the dining hall until we were all at our places, and when they entered, we would — win or lose — give them a thunderous ovation, with hoots, hollers, whistles, and chairs rattling against the floor.

Back when I was ten, we played some midget-league football after work, but the real sport was "war." That fall, The Home was having its central heating system revamped, which meant that huge trenches — some at least eight feet deep, or so I remember — were dug all over campus, especially around Larr's and through the front field. We had the run of the trenches, and did we ever run them, conducting full-scale battles using sticks.

We would mount our "swords" in the asbestos-filled jackets that were stacked everywhere and were intended to be wrapped around the new steam pipes (the cancer threat was unknown in those days). With our makeshift military hardware, we would sneak up on the enemy and bomb them with clods of red Carolina clay (or anything else that could be thrown but would not be life-threatening—although our ammunition rarely hit its intended target).

We would also use the trenches to sneak off to the woods. And those woods became my second home that fall. I would retreat to them whenever I could, whether permitted to or not. In the woods you could do as you pleased. I built a number of forts with the rotting boards left deep in the woods at the old barium-laden springs, where decades earlier rich people had come to bathe in the mineral waters.

In the woods, you could search for salamanders and frogs under the rocks in the creeks that seemed to flow in all directions. You could collect caterpillars, watch them eat their way through a shoebox of leaves, spin their chrysalis, and turn, magically, into butterflies. I've always liked the metaphor of the chrysalis and how the sluggish, awkward creepy-crawlies could turn into beautiful flying creatures.

Along the streams, you could build your own dams, bridges, and ponds. You could fish in a bug-infested pond near the Old Spring House, with a line and hook made of a bent pin or nail stuck to the end of a pole. You could search for puppies left in their den by a stray. You could sit on an upper branch of a tree, look out over the rolling hills and fields, ponder life, and dream of a better world to be.

There isn't a boy who went through The Home who doesn't remember those woods with deep fondness. I remember how the paths began at the dairy and worked their way through the deepest part of the woods. I can even see in my mind the exact steps, some in mud and others up banks, we took to get to the forts we built. I remember the excited anticipation of what we

might find under the next rock in our search for crawdads in
the creeks, and the joy of sipping tea newly brewed from sas-
safras roots. I can still see the Howdy Doody grin CJ would
flash at the thought of a new venture and hear Dooley's chuckle
at the risks he was taking. Dooley would do damn near anything,
especially when it involved scaling trees, even swinging from
one to the next.

In those woods, we found the freedom to do as we pleased,
to test the limits of our minds and bodies, to create, to make
mistakes that could go unnoticed. We found escape from over-
sight. We got energized. We could forget. We found the will to
stretch ourselves and to test the extent to which we could trust
others. We found faith in others. And, yes, we did then what
has since become a fad: we bonded.

Resourcefulness? If you didn't have it, you soon got it.
"Resources" were everywhere. Stuff was lying all around the
farm and kitchen and shops. The challenge was making use of
it. We made pea shooters and flutes from lengths of bamboo,
rubber-band guns from old-fashioned, spring-action clothes-
pins, wind-up tanks from spent thread spools and long wooden
matches, buckets from the bark of poplar trees. We concocted
go-carts from discarded two-by-fours and rusting skates, the
old metal ones with four wheels, one on each corner, not the
modern in-line type. Not many of us were big on skating, but
once one of us figured out how to make a go-cart using them,
another race was on to build the best and, of course, the fastest.

A go-cart can be made from three two-by-fours, one four-
foot piece down the middle, one three-foot piece across each
end of the center piece, with the rear board nailed and the

front bolted so the cart could be steered. A square board for a seat was optional. Steering was done by feet and ropes (more likely, multiple strands of braided, used baling twine) nailed to the front board. Two skates made for four sets of wheels, with half of each skate nailed to the underside of both ends of two wood axles. The "race track," the downhill path that went through the front field, was not wide enough to accommodate more than one cart, but that didn't prevent us from conducting timed heats.

The carts dominated play that fall until someone invented something better. If we dispensed with much of the wood and attached a single broken-apart skate to each end of the bottom of a two-foot-long, ten-inch-wide board, we could then crowd butt and feet together to race side-by-side. Dooley, as usual, dared to stand upright on the board as it rolled along. We may have been the unheralded inventors of skateboarding!

I learned more that fall than I've ever learned in so short a time. Dooley taught me how to make a kite from a single piece of notebook paper, two long dried field straws, and a spool of thread, which would be threaded through the center of the paper and tied to the crossed straws. Such a kite could be sent to the distant horizon with several connected spools of thread. More important, it was cheap.

Mooney taught me how to make toast late at night from bread and pats of butter taken home from supper. Stoves and hotplates weren't permitted in Larr's, but we did have steam pipes and radiators, the large cast-iron accordion type. When the heat was on, the pipes and radiators were hot to the touch. Toast was simple: wipe the metal with your hand (to keep the dust off the bread), apply butter to bread and bread to iron, and wait until the butter melted and the bread hardened.

Chandler taught me how to make a pair of underwear last longer by turning it inside out after two days (remember, we got changes of clothes only twice a week). The life of socks could also be extended by turning them inside out.

Church? That's what Mr. Shanes thought life was all about. He made sure that his charges never missed a chance to go. We went to prayer meetings on Wednesday evenings, Sunday school and regular service on Sunday mornings, and youth group meetings on Sunday evenings. I learned to know God, to one degree or another, in my own rote way. I memorized, at some point, the entire catechism, and then some.

I didn't mind the Sunday services that first fall, but I did mind the ones on Wednesday evenings, not because God was involved but rather because of where they were held: in Little Gary's Chapel, nestled in the middle of campus and named for a little boy from The Home who had died, but not before reportedly saving his pennies to fund a church. It was a dread-fully gloomy place—not much lighting, dark wood, a creaking floor, and blue panes in the arching windows. I remember entering Little Gary's every Wednesday just as the sun was disappearing through the trees. We sang many hymns, but the one that fit the melancholy mood of that chapel has stayed with me:

Now the day is over
Night is drawing nigh,
Shadows of the evening
Steal across the sky.

The organist would drag out the notes, seemingly intent on depressing everyone, me especially. I didn't want to go to prayer meetings because the mood always reminded me of where I wasn't and who was not there with me. In church I felt not with God, but alone.

In early November we were all asked to write letters to Santa, which would be distributed to church groups all over the state who wanted to help the orphans at Christmas. The rules for the letters were simple: tell something about yourself and list three gifts, no combination of them to exceed ten dollars. CJ taught me that one of the best gifts to list was a wallet, because few people gave wallets without enclosing cash, which was always in serious short supply among us. CJ had, by the age of ten, collected several wallets, all but one of which were still unused.

As Christmas approached, we went in groups of ten or twelve to the nearby college, where fraternities entertained us with gifts and songs. There was no escaping the "orphan" tag there. The week before Christmas, Mr. Powder, a textile magnate from a nearby city and the self-appointed Christmas benefactor of The Home's children, would arrive in his white Cadillac. He always brought with him Fred Mantry, one of the first singing cowboys on television, mesh bags of goodies, and a gift for each of us.

We didn't mind receiving gifts. What we minded a great deal was anyone who lorded gifts over us, and Mr. Powder was a showman who arrived in the longest of Cadillacs and strutted before us in expensive clothes, with top hat and cane in hand—a person we saw, even at that early age, as someone who wanted to impress us and take more credit than he deserved. Some of us came to resent Mr. Powder, in spite of some good intentions, mainly because we had to watch his show and be talked down to. That was the string he attached. We took his gifts, but gave no respect in return.

One of the best events at Christmas was the decorating and lighting of the fifteen-foot tree in the main dining hall three weeks before the blessed day. Anyone who had anything to do with The Home, including the hired hands and their children, would join us for supper. The lights would be strung before the evening meal by the older boys and girls, and after eating we would all sing carols, during which each child in turn would walk up to the tree to hang an ornament, some from a box and the rest handmade by the staff and children. The older boys and girls would complete the decorating by draping tinsel around the tree. Then the smallest child would be held up to top the tree with a star.

What is remarkable about the morality that was pressed on us at The Home is that we each were encouraged to drop a contribution in a stocking as we passed by the tree. Here was a group of orphans encouraged to give to the disadvantaged!

Toward the end of our ceremony, we would start to pass a flame from candle to candle, one for each child. The dining room lights would be turned out and the lights on the tree would be plugged in.

The black workers who helped in the kitchen and on the farms would gather in the center of the hall to sing spirituals. They always brought down the house. Mary could add feeling to any note, and Leon could hit the lowest of low notes. For all the years to come for me at The Home, I would anticipate and remember the lighting of the Christmas tree.

Christmas Day that first year was exciting for many of the usual reasons: lots of packages delivered by truck on Christmas Eve, lots of wrapping paper being thrown about on Christmas morning after early church, lots of exhilaration at what we had gotten from Santa and family.

My excitement collapsed that night, however, when an over-powering sense of utter loneliness came back to haunt me. Bed-time came a little later than usual that night. The day had been cold. The night was colder, all the more reason for us to make the mad dash to bed, each scrambling under his covers. We continued to talk in whispers after the lights had been turned out, reminding each other of the gifts we had gotten and making trades of toys to be completed the next day. Giggles repeatedly broke up the talk. After Miss Bauer yelled upstairs for the fifth time in her most serious voice that we would be punished if we didn't get quiet, a sudden hush fell over the sleeping porch.

The other boys seemed to fall asleep without delay. I lay there quietly, my eyes wide open, staring at the ceiling, occasionally glancing out the window to get my bearing on a streetlight in a haze off in the distance, across the ball field. A rush of emotions started in my gut and surged toward my head. I felt flush all over. My scalp felt heated and stretched.

As I lay there, the full truth of the preceding months fell on me with all the weight of my few years. I rose up in bed in a panic, gasping for air but trying not to wake anyone else, not noticing the cold as the covers fell to my legs.

I couldn't breathe!

I was certain that my automatic breathing mechanism, wherever it was, had failed and that if I fell asleep, I would die. I lay there hour after hour, forcing myself to take breaths, trying to stay awake—and alive. Eventually, I could no longer hold on, and I fell asleep deep into that cold, black night.

The feeling started again early the next morning long before anyone else was awake. Again, I was certain that I had to force myself to breathe. Finally, sometime after breakfast I got up the nerve to go to the infirmary on the other side of campus. "I don't know what's wrong with me; I can't breathe," I told the campus nurse. I must have looked tired and worn. My voice was weak. Without missing a step on her way to somewhere else, she waved me off. "Go lie down on that gurney in the outroom. Stay there for a while. I'll be back."

An hour or more passed. I tired of waiting and of having to mislead other children who came through the front door about why I was there. In order to leave, I lied to the nurse's assistant, a high school girl, telling her that I no longer had a problem. But the problem had not gone away and would not completely go away until I was in my twenties. After that fateful Christmas, I lay in bed each night with a secret that I would reveal to no one: I could not breathe. I was afraid to go to sleep. I had, more than anything else, become afraid of death. And I could not tell a single soul.

The Home gave me a lot, but it didn't give me hugs. More than anything else that Christmas night, more than the gifts, I needed a hug. I could not find one, and could not ask for one. That night I realized for the first time, in one complete rush, that my mother had died. She was gone and would not come back. There was nothing I could do. And I hoped no one would ever find out our secret.

Every little boy who comes to terms with life on that scale needs some form of comfort. I wanted someone to tell me that it would all be better. No one could. I found some comfort, eventually, where I least expected it, from a goat and a lamb.

5

GOD'S CREATURES

WHEN SOMEONE ASKS ME WHERE I GREW UP, I ANSWER HONESTLY: on a farm in North Carolina on fifteen hundred acres, more than a hundred of which were given over to orchards, a hundred and fifty to table crops, three hundred or so to hay and corn, and about the same to pastures.

When pressed for details, I list the animals we had: sixty milking cows, at least two hundred head of beef cattle, two enormous breeding bulls, a hundred or more pigs, half a dozen work horses and mules, fifty sheep, five hundred laying hens, and a couple of thousand broilers. We also had a few odd animals, like guinea hens and ducks, running around the barns.

I tell them we had our own mill, canning house, rendering shed, smokehouse, and a couple of dozen tractors (from large

models called "MDs" to the small ones, "Cubs," all from Inter-
national Harvester), trucks (pickups and two-ton flatbeds),
trailers, combines, baling machines, and manure spreaders.
And no farm is complete without its own shithouse, workshop,
and horseshoe pits.

Those who know me are often taken aback, assuming I have
never done any hard labor. I assure them that I am telling the
truth, even though I know it's not the *whole* truth.

In many ways, the farm did define The Home. Life there
revolved mainly around farmwork (although there was also a
lot of lawn and building maintenance to keep many of us
busy). The farm set the work cycles for the year. The work was
hard, and it made us hard in body, if not in mind. The farm animals gave us soft spots in the mind and heart.

The boys at The Home appreciated the skills we learned and
the attitudes we acquired in doing this work—plus the added
advantage of becoming nicely tanned by midsummer and quite
muscular (without the protruding lumps that body builders
develop). People who work on farms are immune to the romantic notion of farming, that back-to-the-earth vision of easy-
going living in rural America. There is no room for that myth
when you have to hoe acres of cornfields in rows that have no
end, and once you've finished the last row start in again on the
first, finished weeks before; when you can't quit even though
you have been hauling hay since seven in the morning; or
when you have to spread load after load of dung over the
turned-up fields.

The animals themselves, apart from the work they made,
were a wholly different matter. They became central to the lives
of most of the boys there, and there was a deep romance in

them. The girls, generally, had nothing to do with the dairy or the farm. After all, it was the 1950s. Girls did "girls' work," while boys did the "tough stuff." One of the misfortunes for the girls was that they didn't have a chance to be with the animals, to think of them as their own.

There is not a boy who worked his way through The Home's farm who does not recall the animals with great fondness, even remembering many of their names decades later. When we dragged Lady past the holding pens at the dairy, we no doubt passed Midnight, a cow with a body blacker than her namesake and a small white dot on her forehead. She must have been well into her twenties then, long past the time when she should have been reduced to hamburger. She gave little milk, and she was dreadfully slow as she led the other cows into the milking barn. But somehow we kept her on. She was the picture of warmth and gentleness, and we liked to think she enjoyed being hugged by us and giving us rides.

Patsy was a mammoth working mare with a beauty all her own: bronze coat, cream-colored mane, a two-inch-wide white stripe running from nose to forehead, huge hooves, slashing but always dirty tail. Her muzzle had the feel of silk. Patsy pulled wagons and plows. She did her work, bore her burden, without complaint. Even when she was years beyond her prime, she remained strong—leaning, her muscles defined, against a harness in the field.

From time to time, we would ride her while she worked. We always vied for the chance to ride her back to the barn. Although foam would be oozing from both sides of her mouth from exhaustion late in her workday, she would, without fail, break into a trot on that trip back.

The mules never seemed to have personalities. They were just mules, big-eared and ornery as hell, most of the time. You dared not try to stroke their muzzles; they were prone to bite.

At the age of twelve, the boys of Larr's moved up to Reba Gorman Cottage, whose greatest advantage was that it gave us semiprivate quarters—two to a room—and more frequent changes of clothes and towels. We, like most boys our age, stashed away copies of *National Geographic*. Occasionally a deck of sexually explicit Japanese playing cards would circulate down from the big boys' cottages, probably left there by alumni in the military on leave for a short visit. But, as farm kids, we had learned about sex earlier, more directly and vividly, from the animals.

The milking cows had to be bred annually to keep them "fresh." When there was no need to build the milking herd, the cows would be taken to the bull pen up the hill, a hundred yards away from the milking barn. We gathered to watch and to giggle at how the bull, one heck of a mean specimen (of course we teased him, from a safe distance), would always sniff and raise his head in a huge bellow before mounting. We were always impressed with the size of the bull. (The cow was, too, or so we liked to think.)

When the milking herd needed building, Mr. Panns would get out his photograph album of the ultimate sires at some far-removed breeding farm, choose one, and order the vial of sperm. The veterinarian would come to the milking barn to impregnate the cows in heat—easily detectable by their mounting each other. I always wondered why the vet had to sink his arm, elbow-deep, into the cow's rear to thread the insemination tube through the other portal (you can bet we never knew the proper names for any body part), but I never asked. I imagined the cow being surprised months later when she dropped her newborn calf.

Birth was always exceedingly impressive to us, that something alive could come out and in a matter of minutes be walking and suckling. Births were something we attended because they were a time for reflection. I watched the process repeatedly in the hope that a great truth would reveal itself. The best I could come up with was that "life gives life," hardly profound but a thought that would do for then.

We were traumatized when the cows needed help, and our efforts at times had to be—well, brutal. I remember one especially difficult birth when Mr. Panns tied a rope to the protruding legs of an unborn calf, tied the other end of the rope to a chain, and then hooked the chain to the jeep. The calf was extracted, but only after the vehicle had spun its wheels for quite some time. Neither the cow nor the calf survived. Such events stick with you. They help you understand the imperfect cycle of life and death.

More often, the animals were a big part of the advantages The Home provided. Each time a calf was born, we could watch, often claim it as our own, name it, nurse it, and make it a pet. The calves were never really ours in the sense that we could keep them, ultimately, from becoming part of the herd or being led to the slaughterhouse (I learned early where veal came from), but they were ours for a time nonetheless.

Half a mile down the railroad tracks and adjacent to The Home's property, the annual county fair was held. It offered the usual carnival rides, but the farm exhibitions and the contests were the focus of the week-long show. We were never

4-H'ers or FFA'ers (Future Farmers of America), but we often joined in the contests with those who were.

Months before the fair, several of us would start looking for that special calf to groom, hoping to be awarded best in show, or even to place. We entered contests not only with calves but sometimes with chickens and guineas, and even raised our own variety of game roosters. So what if we almost always lost? (CJ won once, I think.) We were happy just to be in the shows, which meant also being able to sit with our entrants back in the stalls where people would come by to watch us washing, clipping, and brushing.

I suspect that psychologists who write about "resilient kids" developing "coping skills" early in life might see our efforts at the barns and the fair with these pets as our way of coping with the harm and injury done to us. Maybe there's something to that assessment. We did understand, as all pet owners do, that animals can give as much as they take, very likely more. They take hugs when there is nothing else around for us to hug. They offer warmth when all else is cold. They love when no one cares. They take abuse and keep on loving. And they teach us how to do all of these things. Lady taught us so much that it took decades for us to understand it all.

In the main, however, I don't think we were simply "coping." We were having fun. We were taking charge of something. We were raising another being, and creating a new one inside of us.

A lot of boys and girls have fond memories of their dogs or cats. CJ, Wiley, and I have fond memories of all the farm animals, our goats not least among them. One early spring, when we were twelve and in the sixth grade, CJ got a chance to buy a nanny with two newborn kids the size of thin adult cats — all three for fifteen dollars. CJ didn't have that much money, and he didn't want all three, so Wiley and I bought in for the rights to the kids, four dollars each. We knew we could earn the money from working Saturday afternoons for a quarter an hour (about a buck-forty in today's dollars).

The nanny was a brownish color, more like fudge-ripple than chocolate ice cream. One of the kids was stark white, the other was mostly black, with white hooves and white streaks down her forehead, on her belly and legs, and under her short tail. Wiley took the white kid.

I named my black-and-white one Wanda, I think because of a girl I had met briefly the previous year. I never got to know her, just met her and looked at her from across the room, but differently than I had looked at girls before. Wanda the goat was the best thing I had ever had. You've got to hold a kid in your arms, listening to the purity of its "baaaa" and letting it suckle your little finger, to understand why.

Wanda came to be a pet in every warm and fuzzy sense of that word. I fed her by bottle just as soon as I could. I groomed her, made her a bed in an empty shed to the side of the big hay barn, wrapped blankets around her, swept up the chaff from the alfalfa bales that fell to the floor in the hayloft (she liked the chaff better than the hay), even slept beside her in the shed, which was of course against the rules.

Wanda was not like any other goat. She knew her name and would come when called. She would rub up against your leg like a cat. She would lick you like a dog. She followed me everywhere.

When Wanda was close to being grown, I did what I thought you are supposed to do with goats: I built a wagon for her to pull. The wagon, which was hardly large enough to hold a small boy, was made from scrap wood. The spoked wheels came from a baby carriage that had been thrown away, the harness from braided baling cord. As Spanky of Little Rascals fame did, I used bamboo to make a pole that I tied to the wagon, from which I dangled a carrot over Wanda's head.

The carrot failed miserably. Wanda never liked the wagon, hated the harness. She was never strong enough to pull me, although I got her to try once or twice, but only going downhill. She would fly off down the hill once in a while, though, in an unexplained panic, with the wagon flipping side to side, not rolling on its wheels. I'm sure she was pleased when the wagon fell apart on one of these romps.

What was most amazing about Wanda is that early in her life, before she had ever had kids, she would spontaneously give milk. No one believed me when I said that she gave maybe a quart a day. But I had proof! I sold the proof of Wanda's miracle to a kitchen worker at The Home who believed goat's milk would be good for her arthritic joints, but who was convinced that Wanda had, at some point, been impregnated and had lost the pregnancy. But there were no billies around! I never figured it out.

Life is beset with crosscurrents, conflicting events that on reflection don't match up. I raised Wanda the same summer that Lady fell ill and we took her to the woods. How I could have become so attached to, of all things, a goat at the same time that I participated in that death march I'll never know. I do, however, understand why I went straight to Wanda's shed after the deed. She had never failed me. I knew she would want to sit with me and lick me the rest of the morning if need be.

::

Late in that summer of 1954, football practice started. Then seventh grade began. There was much to do. In the fall Mr. Panns told me that a lot of the pets had to go—there were too many of them. Wanda's shed was being torn down, and I couldn't find another place for her to stay.

Mr. Stevens, the farm boss (Mr. Panns was dairy boss), knew of an auction barn where a friend could take Wanda. After riding with her in the back of the truck to the auction, I had to let her go. That was one of the saddest moments of my life. To people who've never had a goat for a pet, all goats look alike; their faces are without expression. They seem dumb, maybe pesky. But that was never the case with Wanda—from my perspective as a soon-to-be-thirteen-year-old boy. I could sense her mood, as she could sense mine, especially when there was plenty of reason to be moody. She had grown accustomed to riding in the back of a truck, but on that day she was different, unusually alert, nervous, constantly licking her nose and looking around, maybe because my own dread at what I had to do was obvious in my blank stares at the road that passed behind us. No doubt, she could see the strain in my eyes (my sleeping problem had been especially bad the night before).

For much of the six-mile trip, she cuddled beside me, pressing her head more than usual against my side. When we stopped, Mr. Stevens went to talk with someone at the gate to the auction area, which was nothing more than a large tin roof atop telephone-type poles. I lifted Wanda out of the truck, only to have Mr. Stevens walk briskly over to take Wanda's lead from my hands. I barely got a hug and a chance to whisper a few parting words before I had to give her up: "I'm sorry." I watched for a moment as she was led away, never to look back. We left as quickly as we had arrived. On the way back, Mr. Stevens could not help but see the tears in my eyes. "Dickie, she was a fine animal," he said to comfort me. "There will be others." No, there wouldn't. There would never be a time again like the days and months I had Wanda.

She "fetched" (Mr. Stevens's word) $7.50 at auction. I wanted to believe that some other little boy bought her—I *choose* to believe that to this day—but I never learned what happened to Wanda.

Wanda was part of a critical period for me. My view of the world improved markedly on arriving at The Home, but I was not yet settled on a purposeful direction. In those early years at The Home, I still felt the crosscurrents of going with the flow of The Home and not wanting to retreat to my old ways. I was responding to the tugs and pulls of external forces, some good, some bad. I had not yet found a consuming, directing, consistent internal drive. Wanda didn't give me all that I needed, but she helped. She taught me a lot, most important, what it is to have someone to care for and to be responsible for and what it is to have someone—a goat!—care back. Of all things, I got a goat to be my friend, not just a tagalong but a friend who needed me as much as I needed her. That was an accomplishment, a small one maybe, but The Home provided an arena to find those small accomplishments that can build on themselves.

Most of the other boys at The Home had similar experiences with their pets. My brother had a series of puppies. Chandler would find baby crows and raise them to adulthood, training them to fly to him when he called them from the trees and to eat from his shoulder. Dooley and Conner raided squirrels' nests in the far corners of the Upper School's attic. They'd feed the baby squirrels with eyedroppers and make them nests in hidden places in their rooms. We all learned to love our animals. We all had to give them up, too.

Winter came early that year. By the standards of the frozen North, the climate in North Carolina is mild, but the temperature can still drop below freezing. In February 1955, it was unusually cold. The sheep in the fields, many close to term with their lambs, had heavy, full coats. One of them gave birth in the dead of night near the back fence of the pasture, behind the farthest barn, and died in the process. The lamb had probably been fine at birth, but no one knew about the birth for at least a couple of days.

Mr. Stevens found the lamb on a regular check of the fencing, but by that time the poor thing was desperately weak from cold and lack of milk. I suspect it was because he knew my feelings about losing Wanda that he did me the honor of calling me after supper to say he had something for me. With Digger, I ran over to his house in the dark of night to see what it was. Wrapped in newspapers was this lamb, eyes closed, wet, and weak—but breathing. It could barely move, but it did manage one good, loud "baaaa." "I want you to try to take care of it. It won't be easy. She's in a bad way," Mr. Stevens said.

I beamed. I clutched the lamb. Mr. Stevens's wife found some rags to take the place of the paper. We raced back to the cottage. Our first thought was, "We've got to find someplace warm. We've got to get some milk." But we weren't allowed to have animals in our rooms, so everything would have to be hidden. We found the basement of the boiler room in one of the Quads open. It was warm, sort of. We found old towels we could use as blankets. We conned our housemother into believing that we wanted extra milk, which we heated on the radiator. We used our fingers and an eyedropper to try to get the lamb to suckle. We got some milk down her, but not much.

I sat with her as long as I could that night, and I went to her the first thing the next morning. She was still alive, thank God. Again, I stayed with her as long as I could, until I would be counted as tardy but not absent at school. I gave up lunch to be with her that day and the next. I had visions of her making it to her feet. She got better for a while, but she was never able to do more than lift her head. On the third day, she was gone by lunchtime. I tormented myself with thoughts. "Damn, I didn't do it. I shouldn't have gone to school. I should have broken all the rules and kept her in my room." I skipped school that afternoon and went to the woods. I didn't want to be around anybody ever again.

Years later, when I was in my early forties, I began recalling scenes from a movie I had seen as a child called *So Dear to My Heart*. I knew it was about a little boy and a black sheep, but that's about all I could remember. No one I mentioned it to had any memory of it. No video store had it for rent. I was beginning to think that it might just be of my own making when, after a search, I found the video in a mail-order catalog. I sent away for it despite its high price tag.

The $79.00 I paid was worth every penny. The story line must have been in the back of my mind as I sat with the lamb at The Home. It is about Jeremiah, a boy of eight, who takes in a black lamb that has been rejected by its mother because of the color of its coat. The little boy, with the help of a little girl, sets about raising the lamb, which he names Danny, with a single goal: winning the grand prize at the fair, beating all the white sheep with their certified pedigrees. But the lamb makes a mess of things by going on a rampage.

Nevertheless, Jeremiah is determined to take Danny to the county fair. He and the little girl search for honey to sell in order to afford the trip to the fair, and almost don't make it because of one misfortune after another. Jeremiah is advised by a wise (animated) owl who sings, "It's what you do with what you've got—and never mind what you got. It's what you do with what you got that pays off in the end."

Jeremiah doesn't win the blue ribbon at the fair (Danny runs amuck again). But the judges decide to give Danny a special pink ribbon for merit, which has not been awarded in four years. In the minds of the judges, Jeremiah has done quite a lot with what he had to work with. The little boy returns home to a hero's welcome.

This movie fits with my memories of my beloved goat, Wanda, and of the lamb that I could not make well. Living at The Home made me fond of black sheep, those who don't quite fit in because they are different or don't quite see the world the way others see it, who bear up under their burden.

The one principle you learn from those kinds of life experiences, which we were repeatedly reminded of by Mr. Shanes and others at The Home, is that it really doesn't matter what you have, "it's what you do with what you got that pays off in the end." That bit of wisdom was fortified later that year with a young but wise teacher who helped me improve my outlook and sense of purpose.

6

IMPARTIAL
SPECTATORS

MANY OF US ARE LUCKY TO HAVE HAD A TEACHER WHO MADE A difference in our lives, who may even have changed the course of our lives, not necessarily by some specific act or talk but by who that person was and what he or she came to mean to us.

Mrs. Lester, my seventh-grade teacher at The Home's on-campus school, was just such a person. She was in her late twenties that year (which I deduce from what I believe to be her current age; she seemed much older then), petite, although she was taller than any of us, aside from one girl. She was college-educated, fully credentialed, as were all the teachers at The Home (several had master's degrees), an attribute that made them a cut above the standard in the 1950s for county schools in rural North Carolina. She was the no-nonsense type for the most part, never talking in the overly sweet voice some grade-school teachers use and almost always demanding that we work up to her standards, not settling for our own. She was one of those teachers who did not trade content of her lessons for method. We — I — needed her insistence, her standards. But there was something else that we all needed: her warm charm that took time, much of the year, to come through. I felt then, as I do now, that she was not quite sure that children should be placed in orphanages. She took her work as a mission in spite of her reservations.

No doubt, there were other teachers before Mrs. Lester who did their duty as educators, teaching me what they could before passing me on, but it was left to Mrs. Lester to look me in the eyes, to ask me to think about where I was going, and to insist that it was I, not others in my class or my past, who held the reins on my future. I felt she took a special interest in me that year, but other students may have felt they got her special interest, too. With a stern hand and many kind words, she would not allow me to work down to my own gut reactions or to whatever may have been bothering me from my past. She forced me to set the past aside by asking me to look to the future, the one that started each day.

I sometimes see my life as a long journey with sharply drawn turning points, and one of those points was my seventh-grade year. I had passed through the summer of caring for Wanda and taking Lady to the woods. That fall, the seventh-grade boys had football practice in the afternoons, so we were assigned to the early-morning milking team. That meant getting up long before anyone else had awakened and dealing with the biting cold of the milking barn. We found warmth for our hands in the flap of skin between the cow's udder and back leg. Not falling asleep in class was a persistent struggle, one I often lost.

I was starting my third year at The Home, where I had found welcome restraints that I had begun to respect. But I was still looking for meaning in the wrong accomplishments. Several of the other boys and I, but especially me, were fighting the shadows of our troubled youth, trying to gain recognition through pranks and contests, mostly to show off or stir up mischief.

Of course, some of our competitive ways could be constructive. That same fall, someone got a pair of store-bought stilts as a gift. It didn't take Chandler long to take some two-by-one-inch poles from the store at the carpentry shop with the intent of copying the design. He nailed a couple of triangular steps made from scrap two-by-fours to the poles, and *voilà!:* Chandler was walking six inches above the ground.

But six inches was the limit set by the store-bought kind. We knew we could do better. Off we were to another contest, who could make the highest stilts. CJ upped the ante by using the same size poles but raising the steps to a foot or so off the ground. Dooley doubled that height. Bilton went higher. I took them all on, but only after increasing the thickness of the poles to two-by-twos. Up we went, step by step, until one of us reached six feet. We had to climb trees to get on the stilts we made. Staying on them was another feat, especially when we extended the stilt walking to include games of war and contests of who could knock all the others off with ramming rods fashioned from wads of scrap cloth tied to bamboo poles.

Less constructively, we would light our farts with the strike of a match, trying to outdo one another, not realizing how dangerous the trick was. The longer the flame, the better. I was pretty good at it, but CJ was the king. For him, you had to stand way back. Timing was everything.

Chandler, CJ, Dooley, and I would also break into the kitchen of the central dining hall at night, for no higher purpose than to see if we could do it. We never got much of consequence: a carton of milk, a loaf of bread, a gallon jar of peanut butter (who could eat that much?), and a couple of packages of moon pies.

One midnight expedition to the kitchen was especially disastrous for Conner, CJ, and Digger. Conner and CJ broke into the kitchen and left Digger outside in the dark below a window to catch the loot. With no light anywhere, Conner and CJ began dropping loaves of bread and No. 10 cans of fruit cocktail out the window. I can only surmise that they intended to feed everyone back at Reba Gorman. Well, one of the male houseparents caught Digger below the window and forced him to sit quietly against the wall as Conner and CJ continued to drop their stuff into the hands they assumed were still below. Eventually they climbed out the window and fell into the waiting clutches of the houseparent. "All right, boys, you can now haul all of this stuff right back in," he said. "We're going to have to talk to Mr. Shanes in the morning. See how you like that." They knew they were in trouble, and were they ever. They got six weeks of work on Saturday afternoons.

More constructively, Bilton built chicken coops in the woods below the Quads to raise game roosters to show at the fair. That was the constructive half of what he did. The other half was to sell dozens of eggs to the families on the edge of the campus. Of course, he didn't get them from the roosters; he took them from the chicken farm where he, like me, tended the chickens.

I was twelve years old, at that age when I was changing but had not yet figured out where I wanted to go, as distinct from where my constraints would try to keep me. Without a firm sense of direction and purpose, I often went with the flow of the group. The psychology of the group drove us to do some pretty good things, like raise animals and compete on stilts, but it also got us to follow unnecessarily destructive courses, the march at the dairy being one of the more gruesome.

I understand that all young boys (and girls) are prone to follow the herd. Most young boys, however, have an opportunity to get away from their herds. They can go home and be one of a different group, guided by different pressures. At The Home, the herd was almost always all around us. We went to school together, but we also went to meals together, to sleep together, to the ball fields together in various combinations, but with many of the same pressures no matter what the combination. Indeed, the pressures often were compounded. We each had not yet found the grit to make our own mark, independent of what the others required us to do. We needed more grit than most young boys.

I remember starting my seventh-grade year fully committed (along with the other boys) to making my teacher's life difficult, and ending it dead-set on proving to her that I could complete eighth-grade math in the seventh grade. I certainly entered Mrs. Lester's class inauspiciously, my bad behavior still reflecting my troubled past. I embedded tacks in the mesh underside of her ladder-back chair. I slept through many of the fall classes, daring her to wake me. I deliberately pushed girls over in the playground, just to sneak a look at their bottoms (my hormones had begun to pump on a few cylinders). Those pranks were part of a pattern that I wanted desperately to cast off but couldn't quite figure out how. I was fighting with myself, knowing there was a better me.

For much of the year I mischievously asked "why?" to practically everything Mrs. Lester said. If she said, "Two plus two equals four," I would want to know why not five. While such a question is often pondered by high-minded philosophers, my intent was only to disrupt the flow of this young teacher's class.

Corporal punishment, taboo in schools today, was never the first course of action in my days at The Home, but it was never spared either. Mrs. Lester gave paddlings to those of us who were disruptive, and I was hardly the only one who took advantage of her inexperience. She thought she was hurting us, but the blows from her paddleball paddle only *sounded* mean. They never so much as stung. Anyone who has been spanked with a flimsy paddleball paddle by a hundred-pound teacher knows what I mean when I say that the blows hurt her more than they hurt me.

We found humor in the pain we faked and in the pain she felt as she heard the crack of the paddle. We achieved position within the class, competing to see who could get the most paddlings. I won hands down. I got something on the order of a dozen paddlings even before spring had arrived.

It took a dozen for me to get the message that Mrs. Lester was doing something she did not want to do, and that I was doing something I need not do. I saw a sense of caring in her eyes, and through the reflections in those eyes, I got a new perspective on, of all things, me. She seemed to be saying with every gesture, "I know you can change." There was a pleading in her voice — *and in those eyes.* Lady's eyes had also held up mirrors to me. The message in the reflection was strong, but it was not enough by itself. I needed another mirror, another set of eyes, to see where I was not going. Mrs. Lester gave me the necessary mirror on myself.

I remember in bits and pieces the patience Mrs. Lester showed with me, the firmness of her hand, the look of disappointment, the quiet insistence that I could do better, be better — indeed, that it was *I*, not *circumstance,* that was limiting me. Once she got me to see myself in the mirror of her eyes, she got me to believe in another *me* that could be reflected there. Paddling was an old concept that I was familiar with before I went to The Home. Being patted on the back for doing math work above my grade level was something new. I liked it.

While the math I learned in Mrs. Lester's class no doubt influenced my later decision to become an economist (I did not even know what an economist was back then), I also learned that year to see myself differently, as a capable person with an inner direction. It was then that I began building my own dreams.

Why then? That's not such an easy question to answer. The years have obscured many of the details of what Mrs. Lester did. However, I do remember her words one day. I was mad at having done poorly on some English test, and during recess I showed my disgust by moping around the playground, eventually throwing a softball through one of the class windows. I wasn't just venting anger; I was trying to draw attention. And it worked. After having me talk to the principal, Mrs. Lester required me to stay in after school that day. My punishment was some writing assignment, but she also had a talk ready, words repeated with a large measure of concern. She sat in front of me, holding up my chin to make sure I didn't look away. "Dickie, you want to know a secret? My secret is that I know you can do better than you are doing. But that's not important. What's important is for you to come to know what I know about you. You are letting others control what you do. You keep fighting with things that have gone wrong. You have more promise than you understand. All you've got to do is take charge of what you do with the rest of your life. Let go of your past. Take hold of your future. I can help. I want to help, but that's all I can do, help. You *can* do better. Whatever you do, don't do it for me, do it for yourself."

What could she mean, "I *can*"? That was a new thought, a totally different way of looking at the world.

The reason I remember that talk is that she repeated it to me many times. She wouldn't relent. She kept pressing much the same message: "You've got to look for direction—inside. You've got to aim at something. You've got to make productive use of your time now; your future will unfold from what you do in the present." Not a particularly profound message, but one I desperately needed to hear.

When I shied away from reading because reading was difficult for me (I must have been reading several grades below the seventh), she gave me books below my grade level. When I tried to pretend that nothing in the world was interesting, she insisted that I look through a book called *A Thousand Fascinating Facts About the World*. When I showed promise in math, she helped me in my free time during and after school to work through the eighth-grade math workbook, and then pressed me to start ninth-grade math just to let me see that I could do it, if only I would try. When I read something about the weight of the moon in the *Fascinating Facts* book, I asked her about the weight of Earth. She pressed me to figure it out, and while my efforts fell short, I knew she would be interested in all the primitive calculations I made. When I was obviously distraught over the passing of my lamb, she insisted that I look at the bright side: "You tried to help. Not everything works, in spite of our best intentions and efforts, but nothing will ever work if nothing is ever tried." Once she saw me moving with ease through the math, she kept planting a seed: "You should think of college. Look at the people who have gone to college. Think about what they do. Think about the world that it would open."

I vowed that year that I would attend college, which had never before entered my mind and was not a common goal for young people in those days. By the end of the school year, I wanted to be somebody—not just anybody, but someone my seventh-grade teacher might like. I wasn't sure how, but I was determined to find out. And my performance in school took a giant turn for the better once I changed my attitude. I began to improve because I had found deep-seated and focused personal goals and because I had someone to please.

When I graduated from high school, I knew that few of the people in my life before The Home would have thought me capable of it. My aunts back in Raleigh had kept saying how much I meant to them, reminding me often that my father didn't care about my brother and me. I invited the whole of my mother's family to come to my graduation. I really wanted them to be there. My graduating at all was no doubt a surprise to them, but I was also up for several awards, which I wanted very much for them to see me get. I wanted them to hear the principal sing my glories as student-body president (and he did make a fuss over me when I was on stage). I wanted that stark contrast of *before* and *after* to be felt by the people who knew me only before.

None of the family in Raleigh came. But my father showed up—and, to my amazement, he was *sober!* You can bet that my evaluation of him and of my mother's family took a twist that day.

I had sent a special invitation to my seventh-grade teacher, something many graduates did for their "favorite teacher." She came, and asked, "Why me?" I could only answer: "You made this possible."

I sent similar messages to Mrs. Lester when I received my bachelor's degree, my master's degree, and my doctorate. I even dedicated one of my first books to her. Each time, she replied similarly: "Why me?" I couldn't explain. I only knew that I absolutely could not have succeeded academically or written that book—or any of the ones before or since, especially this one—had I not been in her class.

To be sure, there have been other critically important people in my life—Mr. Shanes at The Home, who forced me to think twice before breaching a limit; a college buddy who taught me how to write; and a graduate professor who, by example, showed me how to think—but the course was set, or, should I say, reset, in seventh grade.

I began to understand why one recent Christmas. Earlier that year, a reporter who was interviewing me for an article about my work had asked, "What made your success possible—what made the difference?" I immediately answered: "My seventh-grade teacher." I sent Mrs. Lester the article when it appeared, and received in return one of the best Christmas gifts ever. The gift came in the form of a large plaque, hand-done in needle-point and bordered in red and blue, which reads:

SUCCESS IS
To laugh often and much;
To win the respect of intelligent people and the affection of
    children;
To earn the appreciation of honest people and endure the
    betrayal of false friends;
To think and be granted the right to disagree;
To set goals and accomplish more than ever imagined;
To express gratitude for kindness and encouraging words;
To appreciate beauty;
To find the best of others;
To leave the world a better place than we found it;
Whether by a healthy child, a garden path, or a redeemed social
    condition;
To know even one life breathed easier because you lived;
This is to have
SUCCEEDED.

She told me that she sent the gift because of how much my accomplishments and words of thanks had meant to her over the years, and (much to my surprise) because it reflected sentiments I had expressed in some of the things I had said or written.

I know I have had more good fortune, done more things, gone more places than that little boy in Raleigh (or anyone who knew him then) could ever have imagined. I have not come close to passing fully with grace the test for success that my seventh-grade teacher gave me at Christmas, but I do have a garden and a garden path and I have lived my wildest dreams.

Five years after being in Mrs. Lester's class, our senior class was evaluated for college by a psychology professor from a local university. We took aptitude and IQ tests, and later the Scholastic Aptitude Test (SAT). When the professor took me in his office to go over my scores, he said something to me that I will always remember: "You may not make it through college. Your IQ is not as high as we normally like to see in college students. If you do go, remember that you may get frustrated. I don't know that you can make it. Your aptitude tests show that you have a fondness for transportation. Maybe you should try trucking."

While we boys had, as usual, goofed off while being left in a classroom by ourselves to take the tests, I knew that my results were not far off the mark. My math score on the SAT was above average, but my verbal score was abysmally low. I was reading at one-fourth the speed of most high school seniors, and my vocabulary was way below average. At the same time, I knew something the good professor did not know: I knew where I had come from, where I had started and when. I had enough fire in my belly to mutter under my breath, "Just watch me."

I found a small private college that would admit me (the good ones would not, and Mr. Shanes didn't think I should suffer the shock of a large state university). I gave up what might possibly have been, with some luck and a lot of extra effort, a small-college basketball career, just to prove the professor wrong. (I feared that devoting time to basketball practice would cut into the unusual amount of time I would need to do well in my classes.) While doing the reading for my college courses, I made my own vocabulary flash cards, writing down every word I didn't know on a card and then recording the definition on the other side (my card collection filled more than one shoebox by the end of freshman year).

Over the years, I have worked with colleagues with quick minds and impeccable academic credentials who have failed miserably because they lacked that fire in the belly. They have not moved up and on because they did not *need* to. I did. I had to rise above my scores and do better than the professor expected. I had to prove them wrong and Mrs. Lester right.

A couple of hundred years ago, a wise moral philosopher, who insisted that economics has a moral foundation, explained how people evaluate their actions with reference to their own "impartial spectators." These spectators sit apart from the acting person and render judgments on the moral worth of his or her actions. Some people can construct their own impartial spectators. They know, in their guts and hearts, what is right and wrong. Others of us must find them in certain people who set standards for us, and who may sacrifice immediate praise because of their insistence that actions, words, and deeds be consistent with higher principles. I was fortunate enough to have been touched at an impressionable age by an impartial spectator far wiser than her years, who cared more about my mettle than my medals or pedigree or what had gone before.

Educators talk about the need for *mentors*. They suggest that a mentor is someone who teaches by word and, more important, by example. A mentor is indeed that, but there must be much more to it. A mentor must be someone who does more than pass through someone else's life, or else the impact can be fleeting. The mentor must be someone whom the affected person takes along through life — someone to whom the person can turn, if only in the mind, for advice and guidance, someone who can render judgment even when not around. Someone like Mrs. Lester.

Identifying the core problems of many children of the streets, or those who come up the hard way, is not difficult for those who have lived that type of life. When faced with extraordinary demands on their emotions and inner selves that they are ill equipped, simply because of their age, to handle, such children often become hollowed out emotionally, drained of the necessary core beliefs that hold others together. Children of the streets devise a survival mode, one of responding to external conditions, willing to adjust reflectively to the forces around them.

The outside forces, not inner forces, take control. Children of the streets do what they have to do, go with the flow of the forces in their lives. Their time horizon begins to shrink. More and more, they look to the near term simply because they can no longer see beyond it. They stop investing in all the things that make the long-term possible—schooling, integrity, social skills, the will to do better—those things that are relevant outside their immediate sphere.

Children of the streets, among whom I see myself in my early years, are defined and limited by the streets (or backwoods) they prowl—without the soul (or core set of directing beliefs) they need. They lose the capacity to judge their own actions, because what works is too often the only rule that matters. They lack guidance, from themselves and others. They play every margin, always testing the limits of their external world, and press on when no limits or external checks are found.

Most people have their parents to take along, figuratively, to be their impartial spectators. Many kids of the streets today don't. Their parents are dead, absent, or derelict in duty. Many street children don't ever meet people who ask them to strive to meet a standard beyond their reach, so they never reach beyond their own standard.

I was fortunate to have grown up in The Home because it set boundaries within which we were given a range of opportunities to do good and bad, and to find the difference on our own. It gave us access to resources in the shops, if only the scraps. It challenged us to use the scraps. Our problem was to use them productively, but doing things productively requires judgment and being able to find someone who can judge when no one is around. I had the opportunity at The Home to find my own impartial spectators to whom, in an imaginary sort of way, I always try to defer judgment. I found a substitute soul. I found filler for the "hollow"—the hole in my world. I often ask myself in this or that situation, "What would Mr. Shanes have done?

What would Mrs. Lester think? Would they be proud? Would they smile? Would what I do make them think their efforts were worthwhile?"

Many children of the streets and even of highly advantaged homes are less fortunate than I, and the other children of The Home, in this regard. We got the guidance of a lifetime by people who should have been rewarded and thanked far more than they were. They have been with me—with many of us—all these years. They—a seventh-grade teacher, in particular—filled my void. I found people (and I had to be selective) I wanted to make proud. I remain eternally pleased to be able to say that I could write this book, and all the others that came before it, when my SAT verbal score "back then" was a mere 278.

In the end, my focus on my seventh-grade teacher has a point that is larger than the particular impact she had on me: The Home provided a setting, albeit an institutional one, that allowed us to come in contact with places, things, and people in varying combinations, most of which helped us redefine, to one degree or another, our direction. CJ does not remember Mrs. Lester with the fondness I relate, but he remembers a football coach who had a terrific impact on him. Dooley, unfortunately, found no one, but literally hundreds of kids before our time all point to Mr. Shanes's predecessor, Mr. Camps, as their guiding influence. The alumni from the 1930s and 1940s took Mr. Camps along with them in their lives the way I took Mrs. Lester. Then there was Joe, an aging black farmhand who probably never understood how much he was revered by generations of white orphans. In his own humble way, Joe fortified the message Mrs. Lester pressed.

7

BLACK AND WHITE

A GOOD FRIEND, WHO GREW UP MODESTLY AND WHO ALSO teaches at the university level, once confided, "Richard, you know the difference between our colleagues and us? We know we aren't worth a damn." There is both humor and irony in his flippant assessment. There is also a measure of truth. When I repeat the comment to my friends from The Home, they laugh without hesitation.

Those of us who grew up there have all had to fight at one time or another the conclusion that we aren't worth much. The people who were important to us neglected us, abused us, dumped us. And some of us faced a special problem. It was common during the Great Depression for families to split up their children, some being placed in orphanages and some staying home. CJ and his sisters left a half-brother at home with their mother and the wayward father of the brother. Rebecca came to The Home with a sister while three other sisters stayed behind. The usual reason for a family to split up was lack of income, but it could also happen because some children were just too difficult to handle.

It's hard for a child to accept the claim that there is not enough money in the house to care for everyone. It's even harder for a child to understand that when the choice has to be made (*if* it truly has to be made), he or she will be the one to go. Our family—three aunts, one uncle, and one grandmother—had decided to send my brother and me to The Home, but we could see that they did not send any of our four cousins away.

Our cousins did have parents, which was of some consolation to us, but it still hurt to realize that the family blood was not thick enough to extend across households. Children pick up on those kinds of choices, and those making the choices understand how loudly their actions speak. Some of my friends from The Home are in touch with their parents, now elderly, who remain guilt-ridden. Perhaps they shouldn't. Most of us have been able, for the most part, to get over that traumatic break from them, even to do better in life than we could reasonably have expected had our families not sent us away.

I have worked with many fine academics over the years, but I have also been forced to humor colleagues who are obsessed with their own self-importance, perhaps helped along by their surnames and the elite graduate schools they attended. With their professorial poses and defenses, they seek to convey to others just how smart they are or how far apart they stand from the rest of the human race. They know that what they do is important because *they* are important. I sometimes wish I could feel the same way.

A person who grows up in a home for children and then makes his way in the world doesn't need to be reminded that he does not tower over the professional status achieved by others. He may have been able to recover—he may even have grounds for cockiness—but he will always have a few lingering doubts about his importance.

Where you are is easy to advertise. The distance you have advanced is not so easy to display. While many successful people are able to see themselves as part of the elite, it is damn hard for the children of The Home, no matter how far we rise, to shake the knowledge of where we came from. As a consequence, I find revulsion in the unwarranted arrogance of others, especially when it is defined more by the rights of their birth than by the marks they have made on their own. Many of us suffer from a different kind of arrogance, relating to how far we have been able to rise above the sordid feelings of having been put away and the lingering insecurity that comes with the knowledge that the people who were at one time most important in our lives didn't want us. Our emotional ties tend to remain strong to those down, not up, the social hierarchy from us.

We were always pleased, though, that other people could not tell just by looking that we were orphans. Blacks, for example, who were also in a terribly disadvantaged state in the 1950s, did not have that. Nonetheless, because of our place in the world we identified, in limited ways, with them. The children at The Home were a lily-white group. It was a Christian home, but it was a place that drew a color line. Many of us knew children from other orphanages, but they were all white too. I found out only recently that homes for black children dotted the private social welfare system in North Carolina as well in those days.

The racial division of homes in the state reflected the ways of the 1950s South, and we could not help noticing that we were in a world with strict divisions—not only "us" and "them" but black and white. It was supposedly a world God had made, but with the racial divisions that the Presbyterian synod must have thought were the doing of the Lord.

I always wonder how far I would have gone if I had been forced to wear my distinction on my sleeve, or had not learned to hide my upbringing with a change of dress and manners. I fear that I might—just might—have used my distinction as an excuse, claimed that it was holding me back when obstacles seemed overwhelming.

We did get to know the black people who worked at The Home, sometimes intimately. Blacks did much of the labor in the kitchen and on the farm. However, the black workers' bosses and everyone else—the office workers, nurses, teachers, carpenters, plumbers, and buyers—were all white.

The blacks lived in houses all in a row on the far edge of The Home's property, but none of them had indoor toilets, even though they were newly built. I was a child who saw the world in stark divisions, and I wondered why the white people were provided much better houses than the blacks. I wondered why a few white workers at The Home used the word *nigger*. And I wondered why we could play with the children of the black help but couldn't go to school with them.

I would often be sent to the fields with Joe, a thin man of at least seventy, whose ebony skin was leathery from long years of work under the sun. Joe still had to work to keep out of poverty. Working at The Home allowed him, in addition to collecting his wages, to live in a small century-old two-story log house. The gaps between the two-foot-wide, squared-off timbers were filled in with mud from the surrounding red clay gullies. His home, where he and his wife were responsible for feeding and rearing a gaggle of grandchildren, was at the end of a long, winding, rutted red dirt road that led into the woods of The Home's most northern property. Joe's family used a privy out back and got their water from a well, the kind with a bucket on a rope. You could never approach that house without hearing the laughter of the children, and you could not get away without being offered something to drink or eat.

Joe appeared for work every day in dreadfully dirty overalls, with the ends of the legs frayed. He and Leon, another black worker, would typically arrive a little early for work to sit in their ladder-back chairs that leaned against the front wall of the toolshed. They'd plan their work for the day or talk about church, making light and laughing, whittling on sticks, not to make anything, just to see the sticks reduced to shavings in a pile at their feet. "Gotta get the corn in today in yon' side of sewer field. Guess I'll take the spreader hitched to Big Boy," Leon might say, using their name for one of the tractors. "Then again, I might find me a spot by the old tree, and cool myself for the rest of the day," he'd add, and break out with a belly laugh at the notion that he could even think of loafing on the job. Joe could be expected to add, "Yea, shit, you better get your fat ass in gear." Mr. Stevens, the farm boss, would not have tolerated slack. He had been known to kick butt, but only our butts, the boys who helped in the fields, never Leon's or Joe's. Those two could never be accused of not working, although they worked at dramatically different paces. Leon would charge off in full stride or full throttle to get where he was going. Joe would plod. Leon drove the big tractors and combines. Joe drove Patsy, the mare. Leon's first chore in the morning was to check engines. Joe's was to hitch up Patsy, which he did with care.

My good fortune was that I was often assigned to help Joe, to follow in his footsteps to the horse stalls and sit by him on the creaky trailer Patsy would pull. Joe was steady on the go, eyes straight ahead, broom straw in his mouth. Joe always had time to talk while he worked, whether he was setting tomatoes, picking melons, or following a plow. I came to know him as one of the wisest, nicest, and most generous men I've ever met. He showed me patience and gave me perspective. "Attitude," Joe would blurt out, "now that's what's important. Everyone's got it. Some have more of it than others. The right attitude will take you a long way even if you never have nothin', ya hear me, boy." He seemed to have accepted the world as he found it, and was willing to do the best he could and then some for people he need not have helped: the grandchildren he had taken in and me. "Yea, I love those chil'en. They's what keep me young — and working!"

I couldn't understand why white people were addressed by their last names and black people by their first names. I never learned Joe's last name, but I got to know him better than I knew most of the other workers at The Home. Joe would often talk to me in a fatherly way. I think he tried to teach me what he could. He had had precious little, if any, formal schooling, but he always insisted on the value of an education. "That will open doors," he would tell me. He also gave me advice through his many funny sayings, like this one: "Many things turn from sugar to shit without you ever helpin' them. The trick is findin' a way of turnin' shit into sugar. Now, you remember that, boy. You've really got to work at makin' shit taste like sugar, but it can be done."

Joe was full of optimism and determination. He worked unbelievably hard, and was not given lighter tasks because of his age. But I never remember him complaining, and he ignored my complaints. He did what he had to do, and he left me with words that I can't forget: "You have to put the metal in the ground before you can do any plowin'. You ain't gonna do no plowin' unless you get that metal in the ground. Ya hear that, boy?" More than anyone I have come to know since, Joe had accepted his place in the world and was intent on making the best of what he had to his dying day.

When I think times are tough, I often think of Joe, a man poor in material things but rich in spirit. When he died, I was told, he had a glorious and memorable funeral. It was a celebration, a gathering of family and friends, black and white, who packed the church to overflowing. Joe went out the right way, loved by everyone he touched.

Before I knew the meaning of the word *racism,* I would get confused sometimes. Joe and I shared the same water bottle out in the field and drank from the same streams, after pulling back the long strings of algae. But in Belk's Department Store there were two fountains, side by side: "Whites Only" and "Colored."

Ticket sales at the Planesville movie theater were just as hard to understand. The children of The Home, who got to go to the movies once in a while, could walk right up to the box office, go in the front door, and take our choice of seats. However, the black kids we played with, and who on occasion rode our bus to town, could not walk in with us. They had to go in the side door, up the stairs, and to the balcony.

The most striking division was in school. By the time my class had reached the ninth grade, The Home's population had shrunk in size significantly, maybe to two-thirds what it had been when I arrived there four years earlier. The foster-care system and government aid to families had, I suppose, reduced the number of admissions. The Home's guiding fathers, Mr. Shanes and the board of visitors, decided that the children needed a broader social experience and, perhaps more important, The Home needed to reduce its education budget. We were enrolled in the public school, two miles down the highway.

Every morning we would be picked up by one of the county's yellow school buses at the south underpass (no outsiders rode the bus with us; we filled more than one bus ourselves). As we waited, we would pull gags and tricks on one another, maybe finish off a school assignment, and—remember, this was 1956—pull up our white socks, tighten the rolls in the sleeves of our shirts and the "pegs" in our jeans (narrowed pant legs achieved by folding over the legs at their ends and cuffing), and polish the pennies in our loafers. Our shirt collars would, naturally, be up in the back but the tips would be down.

When we first started taking the bus to the county school, Neal and Bruce always wanted to "match coins" with everyone at the bus stop (we each were given two dimes for lunch). The game was simple: two boys threw a dime in the air while one called out "odds" or "evens." The caller got the bet, both coins, when right. We were gambling in plain view of The Home's administrators. Coins were flipping everywhere. The trouble with the short-lived sport is that Neal and Bruce had weighted their coins to ensure more than their share of wins, a fact that caused any number of us to go to school many days without lunch money. Once Mr. Shanes found out about that, he began to send a monthly check directly to the school to pay for all our lunches in advance. Damn, we were back to being orphans, different from the other kids. A few of us (me included) continued to buy our lunches for a time with our own spending money in order to avoid the label.

Like clockwork, before we boarded our bus, another school bus would pass us going the other way. We would be going south to the white school. The other bus was headed north to the black school. We often waved to the kids we knew in the other bus, and they waved back. The natural economist in me came out: Why not one bus going one way? Why couldn't we go to the same school that our friends went to?

When I was a sophomore in high school, no one in the senior class wanted to lead the Senior High Fellowship, made up of high school kids who met for discussion sessions on Sunday evenings at Little Gary's Chapel. Mr. Shanes decided Bruce should be the leader, and let his preference be known. Not wanting Mr. Shanes to dictate the outcome of the election, the older boys decided they would install their own patsy, me. I was elected by a landslide. Mr. Shanes was not pleased, but I set out to prove him wrong and to declare my independence from everyone, including any of the older boys who might think I was too young to take my own stand. I also wanted to raise a few hackles and to find something I could do that might be impressive and, incidentally, religious.

Racial tensions in the South were mounting in the late 1950s. When I was asked, as the new fellowship leader, to give a talk on Youth Sunday before the congregation at The Home's new church, which would draw a modest attendance from the community as well as The Home, it was natural for me to contemplate talking about race. I didn't want to upset anyone by my talk. I wanted to be polite and politic. The principal of the county school had recently delivered his own convocation diatribe on race. In a fit, he reasoned, "If God had wanted us to live together, he would have made us all black." Those words still ring in my ears as one of the most peculiar conclusions I've ever heard. Two miles away, we were living with the black help at The Home for a major fraction of our summer days. We were playing with their children, even drinking out of the same bottle and peeing in the same bush in the field.

Mr. Heckle, the minister at Little Gary's and a political and religious moderate for his time (I think he even drank wine in the manse), encouraged me to give the five-minute talk I had prepared on race. I wanted to go against the grain, and Mr. Heckle helped me practice the talk but warned me, "You need to understand that some people might not like what you say. But you're right, you know." In all honesty, I think he wanted me to speak where he couldn't.

That Sunday, those of us who were involved in the service filed in with the choir to sit behind the opposing pulpits. Rebecca arose from behind the left pulpit to make the call to worship. Dooley read the scripture, and CJ and four other boys took up the offering. Conner gave a short talk from behind the right pulpit, as did Digger. I couldn't listen; I was too nervous. There were a lot of people out there. My throat was dry. Finally, it was time for me to speak. I simply asked the questions I've posed here. Why is it that we, black and white, can drink from the same bottle in the field but not the same fountain in a store, can play together but cannot sit in the same class, can ride the same bus to the movies but cannot go in the same door? There was no open revolt, but you can be assured that I was unsettled when Mr. Bryant, The Home's purchasing agent, with whom I had worked for a spell, and Mr. Whitmyer, the head cottage supervisor, walked out before I could finish my talk.

I wish I could uncover some deep underlying principle in these experiences or could say that I marched for civil rights years later. All I can say is that I learned more from Joe than from the people who walked out on my talk that day. I got from Joe the good sense to ask questions, the right ones. And I took another step, albeit a tentative one, that day away from my troubled past into a self-determining future.

That Sunday Mr. Heckle beamed. I knew Joe would have liked my talk, so would have Mrs. Lester, if either had been there. Mr. Shanes said he was proud of me. The Home was full of confidence builders, mostly to be found in the things we made out of scrap and trash, in the games we won, in the crops we helped plant and harvest, in the programs we led, in the relationships we developed, in the negative emotions we could sidestep if not overpower. The message everywhere, from Mr. Shanes to Joe, was: "You are worth something. You can do things. You need not let choices made by others hold you back." It was fortified in the great triad — work, sports, and religion — without which The Home would have been a far different, and less influential, place to grow up.

8

GOD IN THE HOME

THERE WERE THREE THINGS THE "POWERS THAT BE" AT THE
Home considered extremely important: work, sports, and religion—in that order. Not that God wasn't emphasized by people who worked at The Home, mind you. He was central to
many people's lives. He was critical to mine, for a time. He just
had some heavy competition from work and sports.

Work was consuming. It's what kept us occupied, what got
the hay in the barn and the No. 10 cans filled with produce
from the fields. During the summers, we worked each weekday
from 7 A.M. to 5 P.M., with an hour off for lunch, and from 8 A.M.
until noon on Saturdays. During the school year, we worked
two to three hours every afternoon, if we did not play sports,
and on Saturday mornings again. The younger boys who

played sports milked the cows before breakfast seven days a week, while the older boys made breakfast. Most of us had our own paying jobs on Saturday afternoons as well. CJ and I worked for a family in Planesville for several years, mowing the lawn, washing windows, pulling weeds from their flowerbeds and from between the bricks on their walks, and doing any other odd jobs they could find for us. They would pick us up at the post office after lunch on Saturdays. The extra work ran our workweeks well above fifty hours in the summer.

For Mr. Shanes, work was more than so many hours of assigned tasks, however; it was a secular religion, something to keep idle hands from mischievous ends. He also saw work assignments as a way for us to learn a trade for the future.

He, the housemothers, and the hired hands repeated any number of morals to us that said, in so many different ways, that work is good for the body and, more important, for the soul. Work is what God gave us to do, and it is what we should do without complaint, if not with cheerfulness, to the glory of God. Eventually, we might be admitted to heaven from really *good* works. We were told to live the Protestant ethic, pure and simple.

In a promotional film made for The Home in the mid-1950s called "When the Bough Breaks," much of the time is taken up with shots of boys hauling hay, laying pipes, painting buildings, herding and milking cows, and picking apples; and of girls sewing, cooking, cleaning, setting the tables, and doing the laundry. All the scenes were overlaid with corny commentary, reminiscent of the era, on the importance of work to body and soul. The ethic stuck for most of us, perhaps to excess.

Nevertheless, even Mr. Shanes seemed a bit confused on the issue of work as it related to the official religious dictates of Presbyterians. We were told by practically everyone affiliated with the church that some of us had already been saved, which was, according to the Presbyterian articles of faith, our pre-destination. But this was obviously intended to be a restricted club. Exactly who had already been saved would, eventually, show up in their good works. We were also reminded that we had to work hard to be among the saved, as reflected in what we accomplished.

I could never fully settle in my own mind the riddle inher-ent in those claims. If some of us Presbyterians had already been saved, and our saving grace would, eventually, show up in our good works, why did we need to push ourselves to work so hard? Those of us who had been saved should never have been inclined to look at work as hard. The good works should come naturally, unless God was prone to mistakes in the selection process. But God never made mistakes, we were told. We talked about such matters in our church youth groups when we, not the adults, were in charge of the programs.

Mr. Shanes didn't have a totally satisfying answer to the rid-dle. The minister didn't either, other than to say, in effect, "that's what we believe." Those who believed such things as a matter of faith were, obviously, among the chosen few, a posi-tion that made "faith" — that is, mere acceptance — a criteria for admittance to heaven. That kind of answer just made the rid-dle even more perplexing for me. Why should we be inclined to question our faith if we have already been predestined to sit at the hand of God for life eternal? I must admit the authorities had me there: I was afraid, for a while, to question religious precepts openly for fear that the very act of questioning would damn me forever—or would reveal to everyone that I had already been damned.

The riddles that religion at The Home presented made us think, and we were used to thinking. Children from The Home were always thinking. The slightest little thing drove me batty. I could never understand, for example, how the girl I was dating in high school, who was not from The Home, could with such confidence correct me for saying *heck* because she knew it was just as bad as saying *hell*. Her minister had told her so. Mine had said much the same, but always with a wink, so it seemed. God would get me for saying *heck* or *hell*, my girlfriend was certain. My minister was pretty sure, but how could God become so enraged over such a trivial matter? And then how could He expect us to split hairs, to realize that saying *hell* was okay when talking about Bible things but not okay in all other regards?

Religion made me contemplate matters of eternity and *internity* (my word for the space within each of us where the mind relentlessly searches for understanding of itself). When I gave my talk on race, I was challenged to find words for thoughts, to search through the contradictions I found in the Church and the fields of The Home. I found a lot of space inside to explore. There were "rooms" to go through, and passages that connected the rooms. I learned that thoughts do not always come effortlessly, that pieces of the most important puzzles of life could be *discovered* in the same way that crawdads could be found under the most unexpected rocks and branches in creeks. The prayers I tried to concoct made me think poetically, with words offering the prospect of feelings as well as facts.

Between religion and work in the order of important things were football and basketball. They were treated much like work; they required a whole lot of sweat, dedication, and perseverance. God made work and games possible. "You owe everything to Him," Reverend Heckle would insist. "How else could all that you see come into being?" he would ask. I have recounted how proud we were of our football tradition that was built on the successes, appropriately exaggerated, of The Home's teams of the 1930s and 1940s, and the pain we went through by having to confront much larger opponents in order to keep The Home in the ranks of the winners, in spite of our dwindling numbers. Sports participation was clearly seen as an opportunity for the poor unfortunate boys of The Home to achieve a measure of the success they may have missed in their lives. Neither we nor the staff voiced these sentiments directly, but achievement even in the small seemed to be a driving force. And a powerful force it was. The success we experienced on the field or court partly explains why we came to call our counterparts from Planesville "hicks." We could beat them. We were worth something. And we were good.

Winning was the name of the game, but not winning at all costs (as so often is the case today). We had to be good sports; poor sportsmanship would not, under any circumstances, be tolerated. God was watching, and we asked Him to watch us before each game, just in case He forgot. Winning—by the rules—gave us stories to tell. Winning was worth memories only if it came against great odds and was pure, clean, and fair.

Our football games were played on Friday afternoons in the pit called Sedgeman Field—which had been carved out of a hillside in the 1930s by herds of mules pulling oversized shovels, steered by gangs of boys from The Home. But most of us preferred basketball to football by a long shot. It was better for those who weren't so brawny, and it wasn't nearly as painful a game. You didn't have to push your opponents around, and they couldn't push you, much. Moreover, many of the football games were played in the afternoon heat of a southern summer. Just try playing in full football gear in ninety-five-degree heat and humidity for over two hours, both defense and offense, and you'll know what I mean.

Finesse was always what was important to me. Long years of working my way through unexpected personal obstacles, whether sneaking into movie theaters in Raleigh or sidestepping the hard question of why I was sent to The Home, made me very good at finessing the opposition in everyday life, and in basketball. You could beat them, if only you could outwit or outquick—or, in the case of basketball, outshoot—them.

Herb, who was our center several years before my varsity days, showed how to make finesse count. He had to: he was only 5'10", a half-foot shorter than the next shortest center in the conference. Nevertheless, with a perfected fadeaway shot from the foul line, Herb could take the best, regularly outscoring the other centers. Herb became my idol. I never entertained the prospects of being center, but I did spend endless hours on the dirt courts and in The Home's gym practicing every conceivable shot, especially my long-jump shot. I figured that if I could not match up with the much taller boys (I was under 5'10") on the inside game, there was possibly some range from which I could shoot freely simply because no one guarding me would ever expect someone like me to shoot from there. I practiced during every free moment from beyond what is now the three-point circle for professional teams, and I was consistently sharp at that range. From the top of the key, I was deadly.

When I played high school ball, I was an unknown on the courts my starting year. At the beginning of the game the ball would come to me repeatedly, and I would sink several straight from "downtown" (twenty-five feet from the basket), at which point the other team would huddle, then return with a "box and one" (a two-by-two zone around the foul lane, with the remaining players on defense assigned to follow a particular player). They would have some squirt chase me for the rest of the game with his hand in my face. If I had had the promise of being a superstar, or just a star, I probably could have taken the one-on-one opposition, but I was never that good, especially when there would be a crowd around me when I got my hands on the ball. But the fact that teams would pay special attention was all I needed to keep up the relentless practice, to the detriment of my studies.

Basketball became my religion partly because it had a fringe benefit: more attention from girls. But, most important, winning at sports was a visible sign that we had achieved something. It was a way of telling the world that we counted. When I graduated, I received the "most athletic" trophy. I was grateful for *any* award, mostly in the hope that my aunts would come to see me receive it. They never did.

Life for many of us at The Home was a matter of creating "counters," of filling in life's scorecard and making sure the world (or, at least, the relevant portion) knew what we had accomplished. When you have been hollowed out, emotionally emptied, at a very early age, denied a sense of self-worth, something needs to be created to fill the void. You can't measure progress by the internal sense of who you are and where you stand with critically important and relevant others. They have left you. You can't draw on internal images of who you are. You don't know who you are and don't want to be who you were.

Sports were better for the soul than work in the field for one special reason. Work in the field could only be counted by the passing hours: the ends of the rows could not be seen and the work could not be ascribed to anyone in particular. In sports, on the other hand, someone was always keeping score *and* counting *and* reporting, even at the high school level.

For this reason, people who have gone through an orphanage understand, to a limited extent, why children of the streets do some of the things they do. Many children of the streets are (I can only surmise) no less empty than the children at The Home often were on their arrival. Children of the streets also play ball because someone, if only themselves and their friends, is counting. All too often their goals are exceedingly narrow and immediate, like how many "hot-dog" tricks (shots made with unnecessary twists and turns of the body in midair) can be pulled off with the ball while others are watching—and counting, not the score so much as the ways the scoring can be made to stand out.

Regrettably, street children's *choices*—in terms of both the options before them and the options they've selected—are not always very good. They deal drugs and fight and steal partly because those things are profitable but also because they can be counted. The advantage of being from The Home is that what counted, and what could be counted, was severely restricted. I look back fondly at my time in The Home because I know that had I not gone there, I would still have had to count. I would just have been counting different things, and I'm not so sure I would have liked the things I would have counted.

The problem with using counting as a substitute for the soul is that once you start, it's hard to stop, and it is all too easy for the count itself, as distinguished from the quality of what is counted, to take on a life of its own. When no one is keeping score of your performance on the court, you simply must find new counters. That's what I did after leaving The Home, first with academic degrees and then with books. When all else I've done seems relatively unimportant, I can remember there are a bunch of cards with my name on them in the Library of Congress. The problem is that later in life you run the risk of running out of counters that mean anything. The void can return.

Recovering what is lost early in life is guesswork, given that it is not always obvious what it is that was lost. Children of The Home (or the streets) simply do not know what to build. They don't know what was there before the void. It came too early in life or consumed all that came before it. Counting is simply part of the guesswork. It is a form of punting on fourth down and long.

I would guess that most of the boys and girls from The Home continue to count, to one degree or another. We just count different things and with varying degrees of dedication. But some, like Dooley, have stopped counting, deliberately getting off the treadmill. He counts peaceful nights of sleep. CJ stepped off the corporate ladder to protect himself against things he did not want to count. Now he counts the plants in his landscaping business. For most of his career, my brother counted, as I have, but in his own way: with ranks and badges in the military.

A strong religious faith was a prime requirement for people who wanted to work at The Home. Work there was a "mission, not a profession," Mr. Shanes stressed to everyone, possibly because it justified the low salaries but mainly because he truly believed it. Mr. Shanes was first and foremost a man of the cloth, one who saw a moral in every event and a religious reason for doing everything. He was rarely inclined to laugh, but when he did, he did so with great flair. His mouth would open to cover his face, his eyes would roll out of sight, and, with nose curled and face red, he would let out one chorus of "hee-hee, ha-ha" after another, all to be concluded with a shaking of his head. His manner was hard, but his intentions were always good. He seemed to me a wise person, one who knew with clarity the difference between right and wrong. He had to take a lot from us and, on occasion, from our relatives who came to campus. His religion held him in good stead.

The few times my father came to campus, he was usually so drunk that I was embarrassed to be seen with him. Sometimes I could see him coming and know he was drunk, and I would run off to hide in the woods. Mr. Shanes would have to calm him down. When I was eleven or twelve, my father would come to campus somewhat more sober, but still with a few under his belt. He would hustle my brother and me over to the administration office, which was something of an echo chamber, for a quickly arranged meeting with Mr. Shanes. (Miss Winfield declined to meet with him, knowing from harsh experience that she could not handle him.)

His temper mounting, my father would begin to rattle off the ways my brother and I were being mistreated: someone had stolen some money he had given me that I had been storing in my trunk; our clothes were not as clean as they should be; there was not enough time for him to visit us; he could not take us off campus for a meal without permission in advance. During one Saturday visit, my brother and I sat just outside the closed door to Mr. Shanes's office in straightback chairs. The argument got heated as my father boomed out complaints of one sort or another. Suddenly he pulled out a gun, just to intimidate Mr. Shanes, so it seemed. I could hear Mr. Shanes say, as directly as he could without raising his voice: "Guns are not allowed in here. I can't talk if you continue to wave that thing. Remember, God would not want you to do anything with that. Remember, your children are outside. Keep your voice down."

I am sure Mr. Shanes thought it was his religious duty to handle matters himself: he never called the police. Nevertheless, when I recently took the opportunity to read my files at The Home, I saw several letters he had written to one person or another (my court-appointed guardian, a lawyer in Raleigh) stressing that my father was "the most difficult person he had ever encountered."

By today's standards, The Home was racist and sexist, but that was nothing unusual in the 1950s. As used today, those words imply something caustic and hateful. But back then the implication—at least for white male Protestants—was simply that

that was the way God intended the world to be. The world inside The Home was not anti-Catholic or anti-Semitic, not openly at least. The official religious dictates did nothing more than convince us that "those" people were not among the chosen.

The Jews' only problem was that they had not accepted Christ as their savior, and the Catholics worshiped false gods in the form of golden sculptures of Christ on the cross in their churches. We were taught that the cross was supposed to be empty and stark, revealing God's capacity to overpower death. Catholics had also surrendered too many powers to the pope, placing too much faith in a mortal man, who was not, and could not, be infallible. We understood mortal fallibility firsthand, in ourselves and others.

In 1959, our Sunday youth group was concerned about the pending election, with John Kennedy pitted against Richard Nixon. The Home was awash with Democrats, as was most of North Carolina at the time. However, the Democrats at The Home, including the minister, were not at all sure that Kennedy's election would be good for the country.

I don't remember ever discussing the candidates' policies in youth groups. What we did discuss was Kennedy's religion. I can remember one discussion in particular, held under a tree in front of the church where all of us were sitting in a circle. The minister worried that Kennedy's election would mean that the pope might control the U.S. military as well as a host of other domestic policies. But then, the discussions in our youth groups were probably not all that dissimilar from discussions that were going on in other youth groups in other denominations around the South. We simply had never known a Catholic. There were none, to our knowledge, in the area. Neither were there any Jewish people around (or, if there were, we didn't know it).

When I arrived at The Home, in 1952, the church was in the center of campus. Later the old church was torn down and a new one erected on the north end of campus. This new church was bigger and better, red brick with a designer's touch, trimmed in white, with a steeple that reached for the clouds. The new Lord's house was one that Little Gary would have been especially proud of because it made the religious life of The Home more comfortable. It was far more spacious and clean—and had *air-conditioning*, quite an amenity for kids who had to sweat their way through every other building on campus. (We *wanted* to go to church in the summertime—just to cool off.)

The church remained a center of campus life even when the building was no longer located in its center. The repeated religious messages had their intended effect. We all worshiped God, and most of us wanted to, some of the time. We went to church night and day, that is, to prayer meeting on Wednesday evenings, Sunday school and church service on Sunday mornings, and youth group meetings on Sunday evenings.

You can imagine the sideshow, as seen from the highway, of young children all dressed up in their best clothes in orderly groups on their way to and from church on Sundays. One of the benefits of growing older was that, eventually, we were allowed to walk to church at our own pace and with whom we liked. We could also sit in church with people other than our cottage mates—like girlfriends or boyfriends.

We had week-long evening revivals on an all-too-frequent basis. Souls were saved in those weeks of redemption, although Presbyterians would not dare show their religion by so much as

marching to an altar. We Presbyterians were much too sophis-
ticated and subdued. Nevertheless, the long-winded preachers
stressed the importance of repentence and being saved. We sat
through practically everything in church other than hymns,
and then we didn't get up for all of those. "Hymn sings," services consisting only of singing, were great—but only because
there were no sermons.

God was a hard taskmaster at The Home. We may have heard
few hellfire-and-brimstone sermons, but we were reminded
often of God's dominating attributes: omniscience, omnipo-
tence, and omnipresence. We came to know Him as a cosmic
Santa Claus with one hell of a temper: He kept a complete list
of all we had done in our lives, good and bad, and was constantly updating His lists. He even knew our intentions. Hell,
we were told, is where bad people go—not just any bad people, but those who never repented. You had to be saved to be
admitted to heaven, and the only way to be saved was by doing
good works and avoiding bad works, or being accepted into the
fellowship of Christ. I was saved more than my share, although
I made the recommitments conveniently, without ever getting
out of my seat, mainly through private prayer.

"Come to God" was a constant theme in the numerous sermons we heard. Dedicate your life to Him. Praise Him. Bow
down to Him. Be contrite for your failings. By all means follow
the rules that God laid down and that The Home laid down.
The Ten Commandments were not presented as God's *suggestions* for behavior; they were absolute. They must be followed,
and when they weren't, He would be counting (and this was
one count most of us would just as soon have not been kept).

When I was around twelve, the age at which we would be

baptized and fully admitted to Little Gary's Chapel, I willingly, even with some gusto, took up the challenge to memorize the catechism, word for word. As usual, we made a race out of it: Who would be the first to be able to recite it all? This question kept us up at night, sometimes with flashlights under our covers. I didn't win that race, but I redoubled my efforts to try to memorize the *advanced* catechism. No one else followed suit. My count was bigger than anyone else's.

Of course, today I don't remember a single phrase from all that effort. I can't figure out why Mr. Shanes thought it was important that we learn not just the principles at the heart of the catechism but the entire text of it, word for word. I suspect that, for most of us, God got lost in the race.

Nevertheless, we needed rules, those external restraints on our behavior, and God's rules seemed then, as they still do, like a pretty good set of guiding, restraining principles, even when they are violated from time to time. God's rules, no doubt, helped to fill out our internal voids until we could devise our own guiding principles and goals. We took things we should not have, we had bad thoughts, but we curbed some of the excesses because we knew He was watching. We cussed, but not as much as we would have. We gave to the church from the money we earned on Saturdays, probably more than we needed to.

But at times the religious zealotry at The Home got out of hand. One housemother required the girls to memorize scripture on a weekly basis, verse upon verse. Why? "A girl needs to know the Bible," was the housemother's reply. Time in one's room was the punishment for any failure to recite the scripture correctly. That housemother would also take a girl to her room when she had done something wrong and pray with her for forgiveness for up to an hour. When Mr. Shanes questioned this behavior, the housemother answered: "The girl needed forgiveness." "Well," Mr. Shanes snapped, "why didn't you forgive her?" I love his question. Why must God do all the forgiving? Why must it take an hour of appeals to God to get forgiveness?

Sex was a violation of the most basic of God's rules. That isn't to say that some of the older boys and girls didn't have sex from time to time, but it was severely checked by the rules, the considerable fear of pregnancy, guilt, and the distance between the girls' and the boys' cottages. God surely would damn you for it. And if Mr. Shanes or any of the housemothers ever caught anyone, we were certain to get a swifter and harsher punishment than anything God might ordain (there just might not be a hell, or so we calculated, but we would certainly be given hell on earth).

Occasionally, stories would circulate about an older boy and girl going to the haylofts at night after the lights were out, or a boy sneaking through the window of one of the girls' rooms. There were also cases of boys succumbing to the overtures of one of the male delivery workers, who would pay for "hand jobs." There were even rumors of a couple of boys who, as seniors, had sex with one of the "old maid" housemothers (I think she was in her forties). Rumors abounded. Exaggerations of sexual exploits were common, as is true of all teenage boys, but our sexual adventures were probably far less common and venturesome than was the case for boys and girls outside The Home.

When we were thirteen or fourteen, Digger and I were caught one night peeping into the girls' cottage. I remember being confronted, as we returned to our cottage, by the news from another boy that Mr. Shanes was waiting for us and was "mad as hell." All we had seen (because the shade on one window was not pulled all the way down, leaving a crack above the window sill through which we peeped) were a few girls' bottoms in panties, but you might have thought we had seen dozens of naked girls from Mr. Shanes's pious reaction and his punishment of a strapping and several Saturday afternoons of hard labor.

"Let me tell you two," Mr. Shanes began, sucking in a deep breath, as he stood up from the couch when we entered the room, "we are not going to tolerate this stuff here. What do you think God would think? You have violated the basic privacy rights of the girls in that cottage, and you have shamed me, the other boys and girls, and most important, yourselves. Have we not taught you anything? What would God think? What is He thinking? I think you know." He went on in this vein for a half-hour. All we could do was get out weak "yes, sirs" to everything he said. We quickly learned that sex—even the looking kind—could be painful. We went back to magazines.

Many of us boys were too guilt-ridden to go very far with our sexual exploits anyway, but most of us had the opportunity to go some distance (not so much with the girls in The Home as with girls outside). By today's standards we were practically virtuous.

The girls, I am told, used to take "tests" at slumber parties, secretly answering a series of sex questions from a magazine: "Have you been petted above the waist?" (two points). "Below the waist?" (three points). "Have you really done IT?" (one hundred points). They would studiously total their points and collect them in such a way that no one would know who won. But

to those girls of the 1950s, who were no saints by any stretch of
the imagination, the *lowest* score was considered the winning
one!

As for me, I was probably the last remaining male of the era
who was a virgin at marriage, in my early twenties (although I
collected some minor points along the way). I don't know
which was the bigger waste, the time I spent reciting the catechism or the emotional energy I spent protecting my virtue.
Maybe it was good that I didn't think I had much of a choice
in either. I knew that if I were to get a girl pregnant, I would
suffer one or both of two uncomfortable consequences: a shot-
gun marriage, with Mr. Shanes holding the gun at the altar,
and/or a one-way ticket someplace else.

Religion at The Home was important for reasons that are not
apparent in the scriptures we read. Religion was a way of impos-
ing an unflinching sense of *responsibility*, or personal account-
ability. We had to be responsible. God told us that we must be.
We had to be responsible for ourselves for very practical reasons: we knew all too well that no one would take care of us if we
transgressed. Moreover, if we did not accept the consequences
for our actions in the here and now, and did not live the good
life, then certainly God would, ultimately, make us accept the
consequences in the hereafter. Perhaps that is why being
responsible remains an abiding virtue with so many children
of The Home.

In high school, I took religion very seriously. I headed the
church youth group for more than a year, organizing programs
and giving youth-day talks. I worked the lights in the church—
all the lights went up at the start of the service, only the choir's
lights were on for the anthem, and the spotlight went on the

minister while gave his sermon—a small set of tasks that I managed to screw up more than once (for instance, turning all the lights off, including the spotlight, when the minister was speaking). I was even convinced for more than a year that I would heed the pressure and go into the ministry. That would have made Mr. Shanes proud—and raised my count.

However, my interest in the ministry was short-lived. It lasted until I took courses in the Old and New Testaments in college, where all the miracles were explained away as ordinary events (Jesus, supposedly, was able to make wine out of water because the sheepskin water bag that he used was soaked with the wine it had previously held). My religion was, to say the least, thin, built more on what others had told me than what I could feel deep inside. The classes were only the last straw in my conversion to doubt.

I had been told at The Home about how God spoke to the faithful through burning bushes and the heart. I would sit in the woods and stare off into space or a bubbling brook to listen for voices and maybe, just maybe, see the face of God. I tried to look for Him inside, which is where everyone kept telling me to look. I tried to "feel" Him in my heart, as the ministers who came to campus for the revivals asked us to do. I tried my best to let Him work through me, as I was told I should do. I just never heard the voices, saw a face, or felt inner signals, no matter how hard I tried. And I've never transferred my membership from Little Gary's Chapel.

Many others from The Home have probably let religion go for another reason. They understand that their lives have been full of failings, transgressions, the things that God, if there is a God, would count. It is hard to accept a God who would fault children for the wrongs they have done. It's difficult to remain true to a God who asks you to bow down to and praise Him, who creates a world full of pressing temptations, and who would damn you to the worst possible fate for succumbing to those temptations. Would He really hold me accountable for my mother's death? Even partially? Why would He dare demand that I repent directly to Him, knowing what her death did to me?

Our reactions over the intervening years to the religion at The Home, naturally, vary widely. A number of the boys have spent distinguished careers in the ministry. Almost all the alumni report that the religious values impressed on them have been critical in their lives. Most still go to church regularly. Others, like me, became skeptics. The God I came to know at The Home was, simply put, not very nice, certainly not someone anyone would want as a neighbor, much less spend eternity with. For most, God has been a comfort. For some, He simply did not hold up under scrutiny.

The great eighteenth-century philosopher David Hume was a self-professed atheist. As an old man, knowing he was dying, he gave an interview in which the reporter asked him what he would say to his Maker if he were to meet him after dying. Hume reportedly snapped, "You didn't give me enough evidence." For me, the evidence has been decidedly too mixed to make a determination, although I remain a religious person. The way I grew up taught me that what needs to be respected are the *life forces* in the world (an attitude that other Home children report they share). My experiences in church were endearing at the time, but they have not been enduring. On the contrary, my experiences in the woods were both. I suspect that many children who went through The Home see life in much the same way, as a small window on the universe, a chance to soak up as much of the passing scenery as possible.

I watch a lot of nature shows. I keep trying to find meaning in the cycles of life and death that are shown. I keep searching for the truth of what is out there beyond the boundaries of the universe. I keep searching for the unifying principles that hold us all together, physically and socially. If God exists, I want, as an economist, to know *how* He thinks (to play on the thoughts of Albert Einstein), if that is possible, by thinking about the way people behave.

The emphasis on work, sports, and religion at The Home, even when it was grossly overdone and misdirected, had redeeming value: we learned some discipline and we accepted, maybe grudgingly and with some hesitation, responsibility for what happens to us (not what happened to us *before* The Home). We were told some things in the field, on the field, and in the fold that were utterly untrue—"You *can* do it yourself, by yourself" (with overwhelming emphasis on the *can*)—but most of us came to believe them.

Many children of the streets are never led (or is it "misled"?) to believe that they are capable of doing the impossible, never pressed to believe myths about what is possible for them. Later on, in college, I read Paul Tillich's *The Courage to Be*. That courage is, to paraphrase the author, the capacity to be that which you are capable of being in spite of all the forces around you that deny your very existence. It is the courage to override circumstances, the naysayers, and the doomsayers. Tillich seemed to think that the courage was totally internal. But that courage sometimes appears to be able to arise from the strangest of all places, out of blatant myths (claims that, on their face, cannot be viewed as very likely).

Regrettably, many kids of the streets—who never get the opportunity we had, to be catapulted into a totally new and productive environment, albeit with flaws—are never fooled into believing that they can deny all the forces around them and, serendipitously, go on to glories they could not have imagined. Their world is confined to what they can now imagine.

It was not hard for me along the way in my career to put together the religion and economics I was taught. Most economists are prone to discuss various policy issues within the rules of the policy process. I have done a lot of that, but I favor focusing on the value of the *rules* themselves, to the extent that I am capable of handling them. The rules seem to be what is important, possibly because people don't, and even can't, understand their importance. The rules are what keep people reasonably organized, predictable, and productive.

I once tried to bring my religious background together with the argument that if God did not exist, people would have to invent Him. People need to follow rules, because then everyone can be more productive. They don't have to waste time and energy trying to figure out what others are going to do or defending themselves from people who break the rules.

The Ten Commandments, and many other rules of decent behavior, are great directives, regardless of whether God exists. However, as was true of us back at The Home, people are inclined to shirk the rules. When they do, their lives are less productive than they would otherwise be. If God enforces the rules—or if God does not exist, but people believe He exists and behave accordingly—then the world can be a far better place. Regardless of whether He exists, if they follow the rules of tolerably decent behavior, they just might think that He does exist (because they are so much better off when they act *as if* He exists).

In the end, I retain the hope that God is not just the figment of someone's imagination. I hope very much that I've just missed the evidence. I hope that if He does exist, I will be found good enough *when the balance is taken*. I say that because I would like very much to be able to see my mother again, to tell her some things, and to find out whether she has been watching. That wish is worth a lot of hope that I'm wrong about God's existence and mercy.

9

TRACKS THROUGH TIME

CRITICS OFTEN BUILD THEIR CASE AGAINST INSTITUTIONAL CARE of children by stressing the confining nature of the rules and regimentation in orphanages. At The Home, we certainly had a lot of rules to follow, and we surely were regimented.

However, the contrast in the freedom we had on "front campus" and out in the "back campus" was stark. I have explained how we all got up together with a bell, went to meals by a bell, and were dismissed from the tables by a bell. Bells of one form or another partitioned the day into school, work, and play. I suppose our tendency to move through the campus in groups with a regularity befitting boot camp probably did lead passersby, and critics, to conclude that we were regimented to an unreasonable, if not stifling, degree.

But when I look back at The Home, I never regret the rules and regimentation, although I am sure I did at the time. What I remember most is the freedom we had everywhere beyond front campus. I can remember the dimensions of the Five-Mile Pasture (so named for the length of its fencing), which sprawled in curves over the hills and holding pens. Those images are as clear in my mind today as they were the day I left. There were no rules there either, aside from the ones we imposed on ourselves. It was a place of open country and open mind.

Dooley or CJ or Digger and I would roam the woods and pastures anytime we got the chance, precisely because of their value as an escape valve. I remember clearly the gates that divided one pasture from another, and how each had to be opened. Come to think of it, there were gateways everywhere on back campus, not just to other places that led away from the rules and regimentation on front campus, but into some pretty good thoughts to mull over while walking with a friend.

Today, I can look back through time and into the mind of a young boy on the roam who is repeatedly wondering what life is all about, peering through the trees or into a pool into the future, wondering where time will take him. I don't think of that boy as tied down by the rules. He sees a world opening to him at some future point, even though, then, his gaze was into a densely cloudy vision. Now, I can see him looking back at me through the cloud. I see him constantly frustrated by the struggle then, as I am now, to find the right thoughts and words to express his life.

As I think about that boy today, he is wondering then, as I

am wondering now, what enabled him to walk through the cloudy future and become me. He would not always like what he would find in me. And I suppose I am more pleased with him then than I am with me now. There were certain steps taken that I wish I hadn't; he wishes the same.

Pondering how the future would unfold was always on my mind back at The Home, I guess because in my early teens I became convinced that there was a future—something I was not so sure about before. A vision of the future probably doesn't seem all that important, unless you know what it is like not to have one. What kids of the street who do not have a place like The Home seem to miss most of all is a refuge that is sufficiently ordered to give them a chance to plot their futures, tentative step by tentative step, in places out of the sight of those who make the rules and do the regimenting. We could make our own mistakes behind front campus, and no one would know.

They, the kids of the street, have too much disorder in their lives and too much of an opportunity to add to the disorder that abounds around them. I now think warmly of the freedom to roam the woods and pastures we had back at The Home precisely because of the *bounds* we faced, a point critics, who have had to look at us from afar in time and place, don't seem to get.

Maybe we benefited unknowingly from the fortuitous layout of The Home, divided by the highway. The protective fence that ran along both sides of the road gave The Home a guarded, institutional look. From the inside, however, it kept us aware that there was a flow to the rest of the world, a fact made transparent by the continuing traffic. Those cars, so it seemed, were going places. We couldn't avoid wondering where they might be going and, more important, where we could go.

The train tracks on the east side of campus that partitioned the farm and fields from other main campus buildings had an even greater impact on us. The trains, many with multiple engines, that frequently came through would strain to keep the hundred or more cars (and we often counted them) moving. The conductors would wave and blow their horns at our insistence (made clear by our miming of pulling down on the horn's lever). We could think, "I can do that. I can be that man, riding along in a train and blowing horns at crossings."

We had to cross the railroad tracks all the time, on our way to work on the farm or at the henhouses on the far reaches of the farmland, and we drove tractors and trucks over them all the time on our way from one field to another. We had to be alert to trains that could come by at any time (and I did come much too close on one occasion, while walking to the gym in something of a daze, failing to notice the oncoming roar of the engines and the blasts of the horn). When standing on the tracks, you could look either way, north or south, and the scene was much the same, the tracks appearing to come together and move off into a bend in the distance.

Going south, the tracks led to the county fairgrounds a half-mile away. At fair time, there was never enough room for all the automobiles, which gave us an opportunity to make some money by parking cars on The Home's property, without permission, of course. The business, which was always controlled by the older boys, was so lucrative that even the space around the post office—federal property, no less—would be converted, after the postmaster had gone for the day, to paid parking spaces. We figured that if the feds ever threatened us with arrest, we could always ask, "Why would you want to lock us up someplace else?"

Going north, the tracks veered away from the highway to a high trestle about halfway to Planesville. The tracks to the north always seemed mysterious and a bit threatening, as they cut through hills with virtually nothing on either side most of the way. Yet the tracks were another path to follow, another way to find out what was beyond the bend that could be seen from the south end of campus, and then what was beyond the next bend, and the next.

The tracks, like all paths, were to be explored and followed, and we walked along them, bend by bend, on several occasions, but never made it all the way to Planesville, mainly because of the high trestle that had to be crossed. The trestle was a challenge to two of my greatest fears: heights above fifty or so feet (and the gorge below the trestle seemed, then, to drop much more than a hundred feet) and the thought of falling through the gaps between the ties under the tracks or being caught in the middle of the trestle as a racing train came around the blind bend on the north end.

Most of my trips along the tracks remain a blur, but I do remember the summer I was fifteen when Conner and I decided to explore the trestle. We started our Saturday afternoon venture on the tracks behind the Upper School. Once off The Home's property on the north end, we began to worry. The tracks were dug deep into the hill, with banks, maybe twenty feet high, of red North Carolina dirt on both sides. What would we do if a train were to come along? We walked fast, to get beyond that part of the track.

We had heard that hoboes could be found camping under the trestle. We wanted to find out what they were like, to sneak up on them to see what they did — if they really did build fires, drink, and tell stories, as we remembered seeing in a movie. Along the way, we mused about many things, not the least of which were the girls we had dated or grown fond of during our first year of high school. We were the first class at The Home to complete a school year (ninth grade) at the county school.

We talked a lot about one special girl, Annie, a pretty girl, not too shapely, hair almost always in a ponytail. What made Annie special were her smile and charm. She was also probably the smartest student in our class, smarter than Conner and I combined, which really is not giving her much credit. Both of us had concentrated on football and basketball during the ninth grade, and we spent a lot of time learning how to appeal to girls by dressing like Elvis, collar up, blue jeans and shirt-sleeves rolled up with, in Conner's case, a pack of cigarettes in the tight roll of the sleeve. We didn't apply ourselves to our books as much as we should have, and we didn't get much encouragement to do otherwise by our housemother.

I still remember Annie fondly because she was my first love. I had started dating her the previous November. I would thumb with Conner or CJ, both of whom were dating Annie's close friends, to meet our dates at the theater in Planesville. After the movie we would typically be dropped off at The Home by the parents of one of our dates. We had to be in by eleven.

We were probably more polite than boys outside The Home because we sensed that everyone in school expected us to act and dress like orphans, however they thought orphans were supposed to act and dress. We understood that going to the county school was something of an experiment, to see whether the experience would be good for us and whether we would be accepted by the community. I always worried that Annie's parents might not think it was a good idea for her to be dating an orphan, so I put up my best front behaviorwise.

On dates, all Annie and I would do was watch the movie, maybe touch shoulders once or twice (back then, a touch of the shoulder was all I needed to be sent into romantic ecstasy!) or hold hands. I got really bold on one occasion and put my arm around Annie—a big step in those days. It probably took me thirty minutes to move my arm up to a good starting position, from where I could yawn and stretch until my arm fell around the back of her chair.

Most boys of the 1950s and before don't forget the first time they put their arm around a girl. In my case, the event was particularly embarrassing, for just as I got my arm in place—success at last!—CJ, who was behind me with his girlfriend watching the whole timid process, burst out laughing and pressed my arm more tightly around Annie's shoulders, which caused Annie to fold over laughing, which caused the people around us to look to see what was so funny, which caused me to turn redder than a beet, even in the dark, and to withdraw my arm in chagrin.

That was the first step with Annie, but it was just about the last. I was too shy—or maybe just too concerned about image—to kiss her for months on end (nine, all told), although I sat with her for hours on her porch swing on the Saturday evenings we didn't go to the movies and practiced kissing my arm for much of the time I dated her.

When Conner and I took our walk along the tracks, it was late July. We talked about kissing and girls. He was not nearly as shy as I was, at least in terms of the experience he claimed. He assured me that girls really did want to be kissed and that "you just have to do it." It was difficult for me to believe him. I confessed that I actually had gotten up the nerve to kiss Annie the previous month, the Saturday night before I went off to Presbyterian church camp in the North Carolina mountains. By then, the fact that I had not yet kissed Annie had become the talk of school cliques, hers and mine. I had to do it, and I did. But after that night, Annie would not go out with me again. I didn't know whether the problem was the kiss or that I just hadn't measured up, in spite of my best effort.

Conner chuckled. He knew why she no longer went out with me after the fateful kiss. "I'm dating her now," he told me. "Damn you, shit," was about the only thing I could say. One of my best buddies had taken my girl, my very first girl, and he did it while I was at church camp. "Damn that church camp," I said. But at least I hadn't turned her off dating boys from The Home. That was the consolation prize, one that should not be underestimated.

Over the years, I've thought a great deal about Annie, more than she could imagine. She was a classy girl from a wonderful family in a nice farmhouse. She came from a place I wanted to go. She helped me move along the tracks by dating me for a while. She taught me that girls like brains as much as brawn and that I didn't want to date dumb girls. I had also "dated up" several classes. Come to think of it, we—Conner, CJ, Dooley, Wiley, and I—all dated girls who were smarter than we were.

I watched how Annie acted, even how she ate. Her habits and manners were far more refined than those found at The Home. I copied her as much as I could, but mainly in little ways. My language and habits in private, however, barely changed. She helped me define my own set of tracks through time, and then to move down them. I still like to look back down those tracks and think about our time in her porch swing.

The trip along the tracks that afternoon was hardly special because of the talk about girls; we talked about girls all the time. What made it special is that along the way, I dared to ask Conner, "Do you have a mother?" which he answered with the obvious, "Of course; everyone does." Conner minimized his words, especially for questions that might touch on repressed emotions.

"No, I mean is your mother living, stupid?"

"No," he said, wanting to end the conversation. But I pressed: "Do you miss her?"

"Not really. I came here when I was four. I don't remember all that much about her, and then I don't have many good memories. She drank a lot and she slapped us around a lot, practically every day. She laid off of us on Christmas, I think, which made Christmas special." He grinned, "Why should I miss her? Do you miss your mother?"

My answer was much the same, short and intentionally deflecting. I don't think I confessed to missing her then, but my question to Conner may have implied that I did. I told him that my memories of my mother were much like his, lots of pain and then relief in her death, which caused Conner to remind me,

"No need to apologize around this place. Sometimes it's better that people die and that they stay dead. Some of our buddies from school are now having to deal with parents who won't let them do what we can. Hey, there are benefits . . . "

One of the reasons that conversation sticks with me is because it was exceedingly rare for those of us at The Home to talk with one another about our painful pasts with our families. We formed a protective society of sorts. Although we would sometimes call each other "orphans," even "damn orphans," we had better not hear someone else at school call any of us that. The person would have to deal with us all. We often came to each other's defense. In the tenth grade, Wiley showed up at school one day beaming in his new London Fog jacket, which he had saved up enough money to buy. One of the hicks at school got the bright idea of taunting Wiley and, eventually, squirting him, covering his jacket with red streaks from a ketchup dispenser. CJ, who was nearby, lost his cool. He flew into a rage and into the classmate, tackling him to the ground, nearly breaking the hick's arm, and forcing him to commit to replacing the jacket.

We knew how to connect with one another to fend off the outside world when it pressed in on us. But when personal topics were broached, our discussions were short, typically cut off by some offhand comment. We might stress the negative about a mother or father, maybe so that we could never forget that the life we had in The Home was better than beforehand, but we didn't allow ourselves the luxury of being emotional with others about our past. The people who got to our inner feelings usually had to dig—and dig some more, with persistence.

But that is not to say that each of us hasn't had a cause to regret that we had to grow up the way we did, detached from the people who gave us life. For one thing, it made it harder for us to take on the responsibility of creating our own families as adults. Becoming a spouse and a parent—a family person—is no mean assignment for any young person. It is typically a process of trial and error among those who live together. The kids of The Home had the added burden of having to fend off the bad images and patterns we held of family life. Many of us knew a great deal about what not to do in family settings, but not much about what to do.

When in college someone would happen to pose some domestic question like, "Do you know how to cook?" I had a quip: "Yes, for a crowd of two hundred, not for a party of four." Living in small groups—families—requires a different category of skills from those I acquired in cottages and college dormitories. And the prospect of fatherhood scared the hell out of me.

Sure, I had models on and off campus to take notes on, but I did have to take notes, and from a distance. After age ten, I never knew the many intimate details that make up family life until I was married. Then I had to learn from scratch that family life and parenting mean more than providing the necessities and making the sort of limited demands on those we love that were made on me back at The Home. Making the most of family life also means more than avoiding the mistakes that my own family had made. It took me a while to give of myself, to learn about interdependence, which requires openness, holds the prospect of wrenching, tearing withdrawal and loss (again), and allows a great deal of control to be held by others.

After my divorce I realized the extent to which good marriages and good families depend not so much on the big issues—for example, where and how well you live—as on relentless attention to the daily details of family life: listening attentively, setting aside time (not hours, but the intimate kind) from our narrow personal pursuits for the family and children as individuals, anticipating their moods, and making a special effort to be pleasant when our own mood swings are pressing us to do otherwise. These are things I learned too late.

But many kids who grow up in families have more problems forming their own families than we at The Home had because they have to endure dysfunctional family and parent models during all of childhood and adolescence. Moreover, there must have been some compensating differences in our upbringing. As a group, our divorce rate is significantly lower than the national rate, and far lower than our parents' divorce rate.

At the same time, there are deeper, more private reasons for regret over the way we grew up. I don't believe I ever missed my mother at The Home as much as I have since. Back there, I'm not so sure I knew what it *was* to miss. The bad memories were close at hand, dominant, perhaps too telling. Nevertheless, I've come to miss her over the years, especially after seeing a child of mine grow up with her mother. I've learned, belatedly, what I missed.

I know fathers can also be very important to their children. But mothers seem (from observation and research) to be far more important in a child's early years, if for no other reasons than that women seem to be better able to nurture—to get closer to and then rear with warmth and insight—their children in ways that many men (me, in particular) simply aren't able to do. I understand it is fashionable to think that men and women are perfect substitutes when it comes to child care, but that seems an odd world to me.

Even if I'm wrong in my presumption, my point relates not so much to *women* per se as to the *concept* of a *mother*. A *mother* is someone whose love and devotion to a child is virtually unconditional. A mother is someone a child can count on for acceptance stretched to the utter limits of kindness, someone to go to for comfort, someone who by the sound of her voice and words of approval can make everything better. She's the person the child *knows* can take away the pain with a kiss. A *mother* is simply someone a child will retreat to (in mind if not in place) when times are tough and can find some solace, just by being near, when the rest of the world provides none. A child who has a *mother* knows that when the rest of the world is closing in on him or her, there is someone who has open arms. Clearly, not all mothers meet this ideal of warmth and concern, and many fathers do. My point relates only to what a mother (or father) *could* mean and what can be missed by children, especially children in an orphanage.

If there is one thing we missed at The Home, it was having access to the type of person our mothers could have been. Mr. Shanes, Joe, Miss Bauer, and Miss Winfield could not, and were not inclined to, be an unflinching source of solace to the children. There were too many of us. There was no natural tie between them and us. The Home was where they worked; it could not endure for us the way a family home normally does. While in college, we could occasionally return to The Home for visits, but permission always had to be sought in writing in advance. The other children we knew continued to scatter as they graduated. The staff gradually changed. The mission of

The Home began to shift. We each, in modest ways, helped the others through their troubles, but that help was not unconditional; it was uncertain, and it was limited by protective shields of our own making. The best we could do to reclaim some of the lost feelings was to return to the woods and the creeks.

If there has been anything I would have loved to have had, it is the type of retreat a mother could provide. Conner, CJ, and Dooley would say the same. Over the years, we would have loved to have been able in those trying times, during which we may have come close to falling on our knees and felt the heat of stress just beneath the scalp—gross mistakes of personal judgment, divorce, failures, repudiation by friends, the death of a child—to go back "home" where we could pace, maybe not even saying a word, but knowing that *someone* was around who would be there no matter what the problem was, no matter what mistakes had been made. That's what's been tough, doing without that sense of comfort that must come from *knowing* that a retreat and a hug are always there.

When I look back at the young boy from The Home taking the walk down the railroad tracks, I see him wishing for me that I had had a fallback position. He's thinking maybe I would have taken more risks, maybe I could have dealt with the hard times better than I have. Maybe I could have felt more comfortable, at ease with myself, along the way. Maybe I would not have counted so desperately.

I suspect that kids who lose their mothers early in life, and find no good surrogate, are reluctant to grow up, inclined to cling to childlike ways. They probably continue to feel much like children deep inside long after they are adults, sensing as they grow older more and more incongruity between the way they want to act and the way the rest of the world expects them to act, forever fending off the demands of the growing years, resisting acceptance of the "passages" of life that others seem to forge with ease. Growing up is a risky venture, fraught with the acceptance of responsibilities and failures. Perhaps it is made even riskier when there are few personal guideposts, or no one to point them out, or no fallback position, no one to say time and again with heart that life means getting older with grace. The young boy back at The Home looks at me with the same sense of puzzlement that he felt then with regard to the child fixed in his mind, wondering if I will ever be able to give him up.

I never fully appreciated the value of a mother—not so much as a *person*, but as a *concept*—until I had a daughter, who came along when I was in my mid-forties, an age when most people have stopped having children. I have four wonderful children, each of whom has had a profound impact on me. However, it wasn't until the fourth that I fully appreciated the power and flower of a child and mother.

As I write this, Kathryn is six, with a radiant smile and sparkling blue eyes. There is no doubt in Kathryn's mind that her mother is there for her, that her mother's love is total *and* unconditional. That little girl has a mother who meets the image of a mother I have been describing. She is warm and wise and patient, always willing to give of her time and energy to the demands of her little girl.

As Kathryn's world expands with the years, you can see her looking to, keying on, her mother for guidance and for solace when things don't go quite right, when she comes upon new fears, when things go bump in the night. Kathryn's mother has proved herself to Kathryn. In her every word and move, Kathryn's mother has said, "I'll always be there for you," and Kathryn believes her and relies on her. You can see the peace Kathryn feels in her eyes, and you can feel the comfort she feels with the world about her with the confidence she exudes. Kathryn has no knowledge of what it is like to have a big dark void in the middle of her world. Her mother won't let the void begin.

Those of us who grew up in The Home lost a long time ago most of those feelings Kathryn has developed. Spouses and friends can help to replenish some of those feelings, but there is still a hole that can never be filled. I suspect that city streets are full of children with holes at their core that are far larger than the children of The Home could ever imagine. We were the lucky ones; we got protected places to deal constructively with our holes, even to fill them in a little.

I understand that Kathryn will face, eventually, some tough times that her mother won't be able to make all better. She will have to go it alone, but she will make a go of it in the comfort that she can fall back and someone will always be waiting to catch her and help her recover.

Conner and I didn't talk about these weighty matters on our walk down the tracks, or any other time. We didn't realize what we were missing. When we reached the trestle that afternoon, we found no hoboes under it, much to our regret. I took a few tentative steps out onto the trestle. Conner went more than halfway. But then a train came around the bend. Not wanting to run across the ties and fearing my foot would get wedged between them, I jumped off the side, but only had six feet to fall. Conner's escape was not as easy. He had to scramble off the side of the trestle and hold on for dear life to the metal beams below as the train passed overhead. The train started braking to a stop. After the train passed, but before it had come to a complete stop, Conner climbed back onto the track and reached me in a run. We scrambled along the gorge and took a different route home. We were lucky that afternoon, as we had been often before. We didn't get caught, and we had an adventure that we could exaggerate with the other boys.

I didn't know then much of what lay past the bend in the tracks except that it led to Planesville and points beyond. I didn't understand where the tracks I might take would lead. My world was confined. By the time I left The Home, the only places aside from it and Raleigh that I had been were the North Carolina mountains; Centralia, a large city forty miles south of campus; and just over the Virginia border.

Never in my wildest imagination would I have ever believed that the tracks I would take through time would reach clear across the country. At the same time, the way I live today remains inextricably tied in small ways to many of the details of daily life back at The Home.

10

HOME LIFE

MUCH OF LIFE AT THE HOME WAS DECIDEDLY DIFFERENT FROM the way other children grew up in the 1950s, but much of it was ordinary, taken as a matter of course and routine, as other children take the daily events of their lives. Daily living was more like a flow of easy-moving water in a large river than the churning of the surf. We knew we lacked many things, but what we didn't have in the way of opportunities and material things were no big deal, at least not at the time.

Growing up involved a strict progression through the cottages, as we were housed by age groups. When I arrived on campus at the age of ten, I was placed in Larr's Cottage, where bedtime was 8:30 P.M. My brother, who was two years older, was placed in Reba Gorman's Cottage, where bedtime was an hour later. My brother does not have much of a place in my story for a simple reason: he and I were never in the same cottage and so did not really grow up together, which may partially explain why we do not have a close relationship to this day.

The boys in my age group became, in effect, my brothers. We did most everything together. We lived together, worked together, played sports together, and went to school together. They are in virtually all of my memories of The Home, and they were the ones I turned to in those times when I needed brotherly advice, companionship, and a laugh.

Two years after we arrived at The Home, my brother was shifted to the Quadrangle, a collection of four smaller cottages arranged in a square, each of which was given a roman numeral. (My brother went to Quad I. I was sent to Reba Gorman's, and two years after that, to Quad III.)

If I had arrived as young as Chandler, two years of age, or younger, I would have been placed in what was called the Baby Cottage. I would have been moved at the age of about five to Rather Cottage.

The first shift, to Reba Gorman's, was welcomed because I then had to share a room with only one other person (not the seven or eight of Larr's sleeping porches). After a while the nightly slumber parties in Larr's got old. The bathrooms in Reba Gorman's were still communal, but we no longer had to wait until Wednesday and Saturday nights for changes of clothes. We actually got a chest of drawers in our rooms to share—*where we could keep all our own clothes!* And we could change clothes at will, so long as we didn't run out before the weekly laundry deliveries, which posed a serious problem in clothes management. Another benefit of living in Reba Gorman's was that we no longer had to go as a group to meals.

However, with the shift, the work became more demanding. When we were on the milking team, we voluntarily went to bed by 8 P.M. Remember, Mr. Panns would be knocking on our doors at 3:30 A.M. By the way, in the 1950s, we did have electric milkers (no hand-milking like you see in the movies, except for "stripping" the cows when the cups were taken off), which meant the job was reduced to cleaning the cows, putting the cups on the teats, monitoring the flow, taking off the cups, transporting the filled canisters to the milk room, cleaning the gutters behind the cows in the barns, and scrubbing the place down.

The Quads were where I spent my last three years at The Home. Because they comprised four different buildings, there were fewer other boys close at hand (only about fourteen in each Quad). Showers were communal, but there was a sink in every room and a toilet room (about the size of a port-a-john) between every two rooms. We were, of course, given more freedom to do as we pleased, but still within strict limits. Bedtime during the week was 10 P.M., 11 P.M. on Saturday nights (special permission was required to stay out until midnight, which would be granted only for good reason and only occasionally).

Like all high school boys, we would have preferred to stay out later most weekend nights, but those restrictions were no big problem. Our high school friends from outside The Home grew up on farms, and they, especially the girls, often faced restrictions that were just as pressing.

Meals at The Home were "institutional" in most senses of that word. They were served family-style, but of the quality, generally, of food served in college cafeterias in the 1960s: nutritious but hardly inspired. That is to say, as far as the food was concerned there was not a whole lot to brag about, but not a lot to complain about either. As I recall, we ate like horses, or as much as we liked of most things—no scenarios like Oliver Twist asking for more gruel.

Most mornings breakfast consisted of a choice of dry cereal or oatmeal served in huge ceramic bowls with toast (made from white bread) and whole milk (just about as much as we wanted). Fruit juices were offered sparingly.

Eggs and bacon were reserved for "special suppers" (which we liked). The absence of eggs on the regular menu was not for frugality—after all, we had five hundred laying hens going full steam most times of the year. And few people thought about restricting egg consumption in the 1950s; we were told they were "good for you—full of protein." We didn't have eggs for breakfast simply because there was not enough time in the morning to cook them for the large number of children and adults who ate in the big dining room, and those of us in the kitchen never volunteered, except once that I recall, to get up extra early in order to add them to the menu.

The toast was the best part of the morning meal. It was smothered in real butter and baked in ovens the size of those in pizza parlors. When I was assigned to the kitchen for breakfast, I made sure that the toast was the best. The key was literally to soak the bread through with butter and then cook it until it was a golden brown. I would melt a monstrous glob of butter in a pan on the gas stove, spread the slices of bread across a series of two- by three-foot pans, slop the butter on with a four-inch paintbrush, and then shove the pans into the oven. At the tables in the dining hall, many of us would make buttered toast and jelly sandwiches. (If the toast was cooked right, which meant that the butter dripped from the edges when the toast was held vertically, it was great.)

The midday meal, which we called dinner (don't ask me why), was a full, generally hot, meal, as was supper. The diet was reasonably well planned and well balanced, nutritious for the time and state of knowledge. We had fresh vegetables and fruits (such as tomatoes and melons) in the summer, but many cooked vegetables (greens and carrots) would be so overboiled in the large kitchen vats that we couldn't tell them from canned by the time they hit the tables.

Meal preparation was often a matter of opening large numbers of No. 10 cans, many of which had been filled and sealed at The Home's small cannery. Need stewed tomatoes? Get out a couple of cases of No. 10 cans of cooked tomatoes. Need peach slices for dessert (which we had a lot, so often that I still don't like peaches)? Open more cans. The girls in their early teens would arrive at the dining hall first to set the forty-odd tables, and the older girls would arrive just before mealtime to deliver the bowls (the size most homes use for mixing) and platters of food to the tables.

With so many head of beef cattle, pigs, sheep, and chickens on the grounds, one might think that our veins would be clogged with animal fats—and they may be, although most of us seem to be remarkably healthy as adults. The country ham always came to the table in typical southern style, often the texture of cardboard and floating in its own redeye gravy, which we poured over the mashed potatoes. Chicken would arrive far greasier than today's greasiest fast-food chicken. Meat loaf was a favorite of the head cook, mainly because it could be made in large pans and cut into squares. Southern fried steak was also served with relative frequency.

I don't recall, however, meat being a major part of the meals (which I am thankful for today). We made up a little jingle that went something like this:

Grits and butter
And beans and bread
Make the meal
That we all dread.

Supper was often meatless, with grits and every conceivable form of beans (black-eyed, navy, pinto, and so on) making up for the protein. Most evenings we had dessert—a square of cake or a bowl of canned peaches (again!), apples, apricots, or prunes. Prunes? Yes, The Home considered the child's whole system, and wanted to make sure that it was cleansed regularly. Watermelon was usually reserved for huge feasts in the center of campus, at which time we would typically stuff ourselves (many of us could each eat more than one large watermelon) and end up in watermelon fights between girls and boys, between cottages, or between sleeping porches within cottages.

Sunday supper was different, always served in makeshift ways in the cottages and composed mainly of two sandwiches (with peanut butter and jelly almost always one of the choices), an apple, and Kool-Aid. And when we made Kool-Aid in the cottages, you can bet that we dumped the sugar in. The Sunday evening meal, which was often eaten in the meeting rooms or, in good weather, outside the cottages, was capped with a double oatmeal cookie (the big ones with the white cream inside).

Steak? The T-bone cuts (and every other good part) were reserved for the athletic awards banquets—an added inducement for playing sports. It's amazing what growing boys will do for a twelve-ounce T-bone.

We didn't have a refrigerator that we could raid at will, but most of the housemothers had refrigerators and stoves in their small apartment kitchens at one end of the cottages. After we made it past Larr's and Miss Bauer, the housemothers would allow us limited use of their kitchens. They would even occasionally make popcorn, though it was not in their job description (many of the housemothers were wonderful people). Popcorn poppers and hotplates were not permitted in our rooms, but that doesn't mean we didn't have them. Our snacks were limited, though, even by the standards of the 1950s. They usually consisted of something we took with us from supper.

The Home was not big on birthdays. The children received no presents, except those cards and packages sent by friends and family members on the outside. Once a month all the children whose birthdays fell in that month would be seated at a table in the center of the dining room, and everyone would sing "Happy Birthday" to them at the beginning of the meal. The birthday kids would be given as much as they wanted from what was served that night, and a sheetcake would be brought in with candles on it. When I had my own children, birthday parties were a new concept to me, something I knew about but had no real feel for. I don't remember much about birthday parties before going to The Home.

Cash was a problem, but not an insurmountable one. Cash

was important for two reasons. First, to buy candies and Cokes when the snack counter in the basement of the administration building opened for a couple of hours on Saturday afternoons (and the prices were not subsidized!). Second, to supplement the clothes provided by The Home.

At times, we would receive money from "home," but we earned much of our cash ourselves. We could store it in The Home's bank, where we each had an account. There was an actual teller's window in the business office, and we filled out our own deposit and withdrawal vouchers.

During my first year at The Home, I learned that you could get a nickel (about a quarter in today's dollars) for each crate of Coke bottles (the old six-ounce size) collected from around campus. I later worked on Saturday afternoons for a local farmer for a quarter an hour (close to $1.40 an hour in today's dollars). CJ and I made the "big time" our junior year in high school when we got a job working for a couple in Planesville at the fabulous rate of a dollar an hour (equivalent to over five dollars an hour today). I say "fabulous" because no one else had such a high pay rate, and the family that hired us was obviously overpaying because of its connection to the Presbyterian church. Several of the girls made extra money cleaning the houses of campus workers.

I supplemented my income from these jobs with a paper route (which I bought from CJ), delivering the local Planesville paper to about two dozen customers on the edge of campus. I also sold shoes by mail, but I gave that up when I sold only two pairs in six months.

My big break came when I took up cutting the boys' hair, for which The Home paid me at a rate of a dime per head (because the haircutting was over and above the normal workload). Those barber skills came in handy in college, when I set up shop three afternoons a week and cut as many as twelve heads (which is what I called the haircuts) an hour. I charged only fifty cents then, but in today's dollars, I probably averaged between fifteen and twenty dollars an hour, enough to cover a lot of college living expenses. I estimate that I cut over five thousand heads while in college.

Transportation was always a problem for us, so we did not go many places when we were young. Life on campus was pretty much it, aside from the occasional shopping or movie trip to Planesville. When we did go off campus when we were young, we almost always took the green bus. When we were older, say, in high school, we thumbed to town, lining up for rides every Saturday afternoon at the post office beside the highway. On the way back, we would line up at the bus stop in Planesville.

Hitching a ride was not difficult in North Carolina in the 1950s, and there was virtually no threat of violence. However, the trip in and out of town was not without some concern. There were some homosexual men who would sometimes prowl the highway looking for boys, and they knew our thumbing spots. You had to watch out for Blow Job Joe, our name for one person who gave rides and was particularly persistent and frequently on the prowl. When we could spot him, we would wave him on. I had to get out of his car more than once and walk the rest of the way to or from town, but those were the costs of getting where you needed to go. (Not many gays had dared to come out of the closet in those days, which means we encountered only those who preyed on young boys.)

By the time we were fourteen or fifteen, practically all the boys learned to drive—on tractors. We would start out on "Cubs" and advance to the bigger tractors and then to pickups and two-ton flatbeds. As soon as we turned sixteen, we'd get our licenses, which meant mainly that we could do more advanced forms of work around The Home, for example, taking milk to be sold to the dairy in Planesville.

The girls, however, were a different story. They were never taught to drive, which means that they did not get their licenses until after they left The Home. Rebecca did not learn how to drive until she was twenty-five, and then had to pay a driving instructor. She and other girls relate how confining the lack of a driver's license was, even in the 1950s and 1960s.

Clare, CJ's sister, who had a figure fit for boys' locker-room calendars, relates how the girls had to make do with hand-me-down bras. It was difficult for the girls to obtain makeup and then to learn how to use it properly. Several of the house-mothers discouraged its use, even among the older high school girls, and had little time to spend on such matters.

We boys could not have our own cars, even if we could have afforded them, which we couldn't. However, on extraordinarily rare occasions, say, prom night, we would be given the keys to one of The Home's station wagons, a policy that was introduced only after we started going to the county high school. That privilege was halted for a while when one boy wrecked the station wagon and had the bright idea of trying to hide it.

In the ninth grade, I often thumbed to town to meet Annie, my first love, at the movie theater where her father would drop her off. At other times, I rode my bike the five miles to her house, which was on a winding back road. The trip there was not bad, but it was tough getting home in the pitch-dark. I could barely see the road ahead, and drivers could barely see me.

Our best bet in later years was to date someone outside The Home who had access to a car. I dated a girl my senior year who had her own new pink (yes, it was pink with gray trim) Mercury, fins and all. I had all the transportation I needed that year, since the girl's mother had started filling a hope chest for her.

One of the best things about growing up in the rural South was that there were always a lot of parking places. And The Home had some of the finest parking places in the county because it was private property, so we would be left undisturbed by patrols.

The girls were on the other side of campus. They worked in the laundry (where one of the girls got her hand caught and fried in a sheet press when she was in the eighth grade) and in the sewing room above the laundry, where they did the mending and made many of the dresses for the girls on campus (some of the dresses were made out of patterned feed sacks — designed for that purpose for farm families by the milling companies).

The girls faced far more severe restrictions than we boys did. They had to sign out to go practically everywhere (for example, the gym or the snack counter). They could not thumb to town (times were safe, but not that safe). They had to be in earlier than we did. Indeed, Rebecca relates that Mr. Shanes would go so far as to interview boys from off campus who wanted to date one of the girls of the Home, just to make sure their intentions were "pure."

Since we didn't grow up with girls, even our own sisters — they were always on the other side of campus — we boys developed unrealistic expectations about girls and women. And the religious training we received put them in a special, elevated place (after all, they were "givers of life").

There was no choice about clothes in the early years. You simply wore what was handed to you on Wednesdays and Saturdays (or, if you complained, suffered the grousing of Miss Bauer). Later, you could choose a specified number of shirts, jeans, socks, and so on from the stash of goods in the basement of the administration building. The Home's buyer would determine the array of choices, and we would simply walk among the boxes and pick out what we wanted. The process was nothing like a shopping trip; it was, basically, in and out with a bag to carry back to the cottage. When we were juniors, The Home took all of us boys to a men's store in Planesville to buy our first suit. Only limited attention was paid to making the suits fit, though, since we wore them sparingly, mainly to church.

We supplemented our wardrobes with things sent from home and, it pains me to say, shoplifting. Although most of our best clothes were bought with money we earned, many of us continued our crooked ways, all too successfully. Not long ago I called CJ about getting together in Planesville, and he could not help reminding me of our old ways. "Dickie," he said, "no need to meet at the restaurant. Let's meet at Belk's. You take the back half, I'll take the front half, and we'll divide the booty!" Some things are hard to live down.

Television was new in the 1950s. We had one of the first, primitive sets in the downstairs hall of Larr's Cottage in 1953, a church donation. There wasn't much more than Howdy Doody and singing cowboys to watch in those days, but we wouldn't miss the chance to watch, regardless of what was on. We'd sit on the floor, transfixed.

Reba Gorman's and the Quads had television sets, too, but the chairs in the TV rooms had hard bottoms and backs. There was only one cottage on campus then with real living room–type furniture (something other than the institutional hard sofas with metal bars on the ends), and it happened to be our Quad. That was a nice room. After I left The Home, whenever I moved to a new place, I have had a compulsion to immediately unpack and set up the furniture. I seek comfort in the furniture and sense of place.

We got our own radios, either from earnings or as Christmas presents. Several of us assembled small crystal-based radios from kits. I can remember getting my first fully assembled radio from the Sears catalog when I was in the ninth grade. It was small, less than half the size of a loaf of bread, and it was, by the standards of the worst radio today, poor, but "Don't Be Cruel" has never sounded better.

Most of the children spent two weeks away from The Home in the summer. They went back to where they came from, and their families might then take them someplace else. The biggest benefit was having two weeks in the height of summer when we did not have to work. A number of kids, including me, chose not to go "home" for vacation. Some, like me, whose connections to family members were strained or tenuous, found vacation troublesome. Others found it difficult readjusting to life at The Home after vacation, since they had to leave behind any rekindled family feelings. Occasionally, kids would not return to The Home.

Those children who had no place to go or did not want to

go home all stayed in one cottage for the two weeks. There would be some entertainment for us—a trip to the movies, for example—but it was mainly a few days of rest. I liked it, primarily because I could sleep in and do what I wanted during the days without so many kids around. Even then, I tended to spend the time with friends on and off campus, not with my brother. I also liked not having to deal with my dad's drunkenness and incessant traveling around the back roads of North Carolina looking for work, which had always been a problem when my brother and I spent time with him.

Come September, it was back to school, like all kids. While doing well in school was considered important, frankly, the emphasis on studying was minimal, more rhetoric than reality. We had access to the library in the old high school on campus, but I don't remember making much use of it. To be honest, I don't remember spending a lot of time studying at night. Neither do many of my buddies. There was not a whole lot of time left at the end of the day, after work and sports. Worst of all, I did little reading, not that there was much around to read—no newspapers or magazines, and few books.

In other areas, The Home probably provided services well above average for the time. Our medical and dental care was about as complete as possible. We had what must have been a forty-bed infirmary on campus (boys' room on one side and girls' room on the other, of course), staffed by a full-time registered nurse, and doctors were on call. We got annual checkups, but mainly of the down-and-dirty type: "Turn your head to the side and cough. Next."

We had our own fully equipped dental office on the second

floor of the infirmary. The dentist would work on campus two or three days a week. And we needed him, since we did not fully comply with the rules on brushing our teeth after every meal. Some of us, including me, had buck teeth. No problem. The orthodontist fixed us up with braces for a couple of years. I broke off half of a front tooth at age twelve while playing rag tag: being pursued at dusk, I stupidly ran into the basement of Reba Gorman's Cottage, which is filled with metal support columns, cut the light, and continued running in total darkness. *That* was a problem. My broken tooth wasn't fixed for several years.

Overall, though, when it came to medical care, we had nothing to complain about. We were healthier than average, and I attribute my remaining good health to my years of work, sports, and decent diet at The Home. Most of us today are trim and fit, not by the standards of, say, California beaches, but certainly by the standards of rural North Carolina.

Punishment of any kind at The Home was rare, but it could be harsh when it did occur, often leaving a lasting impression on those who were punished. However, the *threat* of punishment was constant, a way to keep things orderly.

The paddling I described my classmates and me getting in the seventh grade was mild, something of a joke. Some punishment involved nothing more than being required to stand in a corner, stay in our rooms for a period of time, or write "I will not do [whatever the offense was]" 100,000 times, or so it seemed.

Regardless of its form, the punishment typically escalated with repeat offenses. Mr. Shanes was an economist in this regard.

He understood that there is some price (severity of punishment) for wrongdoing that would, eventually, cause kids to stop it.

Much punishment involved work, mainly assignments on Saturday afternoons, the only afternoon (except Sunday) we were freed from regular chores. We might be given duties like washing windows, cleaning the grout between the bathroom tiles with a toothbrush, or hoeing additional fields of corn (which may or may not have needed hoeing). Or we could be given the least favored assignments, from kitchen duties to sewer duties. The more serious punishments might include the revoking of thumbing or sports privileges.

You learned early at The Home not to get on the bad side of anyone in authority, which would mean more frequent and more severe forms of punishment. Few appeals were allowed. Each hired person had his own methods. The farm boss, for example, often took to kicking boys in the butt if he caught them loafing (and in the right position).

Sneaking off to the woods or to town without permission could get you several hours of work on Saturday afternoons. For girls, sneaking out at night after the lights were out could mean weeks in their rooms and no dating privileges. Not working as hard as one was expected to could add more hours of work.

The most serious threat of all hung constantly over our heads: being sent to Jackson Training School, the state detention center for juvenile offenders. We were told the most vile things about the place, how the boys there lived in cells, were fed little, and were made to work even harder than we were. I never knew anyone who actually was sent there, but the dismal prospect was enough to keep most of us from pressing the limits of the powers that be. I can still hear Miss Bauer and Mr. Whitmyer saying, "If you want to be sent to Jackson, then just keep doing what you are doing. I will pack your bags. If you think things are tough here, wait until you go there."

Of course, many of us were just as afraid of being sent back to where we came from. That was a real motivator for many children of The Home, including me. We all knew of recalcitrant kids who had been "sent away."

In most regards, the standards for punishment were probably no more severe than the punishment meted out in run-of-the-mill homes in the outside world in the 1950s. I remember the whippings I got before going to The Home as clearly as I remember the belt lashing Conner and I got from Mr. Panns at the dairy for letting the cows onto front campus in the middle of the night. The main difference is that Mr. Panns's belt was wider and longer than any belt I had been hit with before The Home, and he was far stronger than my mother, father, or aunts.

Punishment, even corporal punishment, was common inside or outside The Home in those days. People just didn't spare the rod (or belt or switches). Trying to reason with children was not widely employed in child management, as I recollect.

One person who worked at The Home is remembered for his punishment, and only for that. None of us has a memory of him that does not, in one way or another, involve serious punishment or revenge. We called him Mr. Bowtie, or just Bowtie, because he always wore long-sleeved white shirts and bowties, no matter what the weather or circumstance. He was a stocky, cocky, retired master sergeant, with his hair trimmed to the skin on the sides. Bowtie was hired to supervise the boys and their housemothers and, I suppose, to regiment the place further than it already was. He was a mean son of a bitch.

I don't think he ever smiled, and he always walked in a rush, as if he had someplace important to go, which he didn't. Bowtie wanted us to act like little military recruits, obeying his every command. If we didn't, he would, as CJ put it, "beat the hell out of us."

Neal, who is now a headmaster of a private school, was one of his most frequent victims. On one occasion, Neal, who was sixteen at the time, had sneaked off to town. When he returned, Bowtie was waiting with two of the hired farmworkers and a three-inch-wide strap that, when doubled, was still five feet long. Bowtie could make Singapore's practice of caning look like child's play. In typical fashion, he had the two hired hands hold Neal down and then swung the strap across the boy's bare buttocks, again and again, drawing blood. Indeed, we wondered whether he used the sight of blood as a sign to stop.

Some of the boys still have scars on their buttocks, and in their memories. To think that Bowtie got by with what he did for as long as he did, when his bad treatment of the boys should have been apparent all along to Mr. Shanes, mystifies and infuriates me. No one deserved the treatment Bowtie dished out, least of all Rendall, whose assessment of his Home experience remains, on balance, positive. Rendall, now a hospital administrator, has told so many Home stories at work that his hospital parking space has his name followed by "RO" (for "Registered Orphan"). He is particularly proud of the story he tells, with terrific flair, about how he got the best of Bowtie.

In the late 1950s the television program *Zorro* was popular, so popular that teenagers would make Zorro's signature in stretched-out Z's everywhere. Swish, swish, swish, and the Z would be etched on the ground, sidewalk, or wall.

The program inspired Rendall and Chandler with a plan. They would climb up the hundred-foot silver water tower on campus, immediately behind the dining hall, and paint Z-O-R-R-O in three-foot black letters, with the bottom of the Z swishing under the rest of the letters (as was always done in the TV program). The conspirators, fifteen and sixteen at the time, took paint and brushes from the carpentry shop. They got up around 4 A.M., sneaked out of their Quad (the one where Bowtie lived), stole their way across campus, and scaled the tower. They could barely see what they were doing, but they painted with all the skill of modern-day graffiti artists.

Their handiwork became evident with the light of day. Everyone on campus could see what they had done on the way to breakfast. Every driver could see their prank from the highway that went through campus. Bowtie was madder than hell. His face was beet-red throughout breakfast, as though someone had drawn his bowtie far too tight. He was barely able to talk to anyone, not even at that time able to ask who did it. His authority had been challenged, which was exactly the point. We wanted to taunt him so badly that he would break and even Mr. Shanes, who favored corporal punishment to a degree, would no longer be able to accept Bowtie's harsh punishment.

After school, Bowtie called all the boys together in the gym for a lecture. He was determined to find the culprit. He started his lecture calmly, but, as he was prone to do, he quickly reached a first-alert anger stage. Brandishing his strap, he threatened us all with severe punishment if the villain or villains were not revealed. No one broke.

Bowtie threatened us with even worse punishment if the water tower were ever painted again. The threat of the culprit being sent to Jackson Training School was, of course, made with unusual clarity. Our honor code, however, still held.

Bowtie reluctantly had the letters painted over (he really wanted to have the culprits do the repainting), and, knowing that his honor and authority would surely be challenged again, he then paid two boys to stand guard all night to prevent anyone from repeating the prank. Well, the threats and precautions were all the challenge Rendall and Chandler needed.

Rendall remembers how he and Chandler set their alarm clock for 2:30 in the morning, sneaked out, found the guards sound asleep under covers at the base of the water tower, went back up the tower, and painted in even bigger letters: "Z-O-R-R-O Rides Again." Then, they added a huge polka-dotted bowtie at the end. Rendall says that one of the proudest moments of his life came when everyone, but especially Bowtie, saw their deed in full view on the way to breakfast the next morning.

Bowtie had been had! And he was more livid than ever. Mr. Shanes now got into the middle of matters, calling another meeting, and both he and Bowtie described the punishments that would befall us if the culprit were not revealed. But no one said a word.

The day after the water tower was again painted over, Rendall was back at his after-school duties in the carpentry shop, when Mr. Unwin, who ran the shop, began a commentary on the recent campus events. In the slowests of southern drawls, Mr. Unwin said as he stared up at the ceiling and rubbed the underside of his double chin: "Well, isn't it interesting that I'm missing a can of paint the exact same color as the paint on that water tower up there? I just can't figure where that can of paint is. Oh well, I'm sure it will turn up somewhere." Then, turning to Rendall: "Won't it, Rendall?"

If Mr. Unwin had let on what he knew, there's no telling what would have happened to Rendall. It's a sure bet that he would not have lasted long at The Home and, for that reason, might not be the hospital administrator and "RO" that he is today.

Ronnie, another boy I knew at The Home, who now sells insurance, remains proud of his efforts to rid the campus of the scourge of Bowtie. At the age of sixteen, Ronnie repeatedly left his room messy. Bowtie had had it. He gave Ronnie one of his signature, butt-bruising strappings. The beating was so hard that Ronnie decided he could not take it anymore (it was not his first beating). He ran away that evening. He was found a few days later at his former home, several hundred miles away, by Mr. Shanes, who had come to investigate what had happened (mainly because Ronnie was a star on the football team and unlikely to run away). Ronnie showed Mr. Shanes the marks that were still evident and told him that he would not return while Bowtie remained at The Home.

Mr. Shanes was visibly shaken by what he saw, and fired Bowtie. The whole campus had gotten a form of revenge, and Ronnie came back.

A major factor with raising children in any setting is the adults who care for them. It is true of both families and foster homes. It was certainly true at The Home. For the most part, the people who worked there were good, often wonderful, people. They were kind and, to an extent, caring. People like Miss Winfield could be especially caring. Bowtie was truly the exception. Mrs. Kay, who was my housemother for the three years I lived at the Quads, and who made more cookies for us at her own expense than she should have, sent me a birthday card every year after I left The Home until she died, in her late eighties. She was the only person in the world who would have thought to do that. My aunts had stopped sending cards when I was in my early teens.

The Home should not be condemned because of its few bad apples, and Bowtie was certainly the worst. In the long run, what's in the whole bushel is what counts. That's what we who lived at The Home have looked at, and that's why so many of us look back at it with fondness.

At some point, life in the real world beyond The Home's fence had to begin. We were all warned early in our senior year of high school that graduation night would be our last night at The Home. How could we prepare ourselves for that? When graduation day came and the ceremony was over, I remember dashing into the rest room in an outpouring of emotion and tears. I was overwhelmed by thoughts of who had and had not attended my graduation, what was said about me in the ceremony, and the changes that were pending in my life. The thought of jumping into a new world by myself terrified me.

A couple of the boys had already signed up for one of the military services. I, like several others, had gotten a job in a nearby town. I would be working on the maintenance crew of a company that sold large road-working machinery. I had also gotten a room in Planesville in the home of a nice little old lady who always kept one boarder, and who was the aunt of my girlfriend at the time. After I moved in, I couldn't believe how quiet my room was. *There was no one else around.*

My task that summer was to save as much money as possible to contribute to my college education. The great luxury of growing up in The Home, beginning in the late 1950s, was that if you wanted to go to college, could get accepted to one, and would do what you could to help pay the bills, The Home would pay the rest—for both boys and girls, although the boys probably got more encouragement to go on to college. Most of us got some form of college education with substantial support from The Home.

From my work in the summers and while in college, I covered most of the costs of my clothes, books, supplies, laundry, and entertainment. The Home covered tuition, lab fees, and room and board, beyond what was covered by a small scholarship I received and my savings.

We could go back to The Home for short stays during college. For the first couple of years, I would go back on Christmas break. I could get a place to sleep after working all day in Planesville for a men's clothing store. However, all of us gradually moved on and found other places to stay during breaks. I often stayed with a very nice couple in a small town south of Centralia. CJ often stayed with a family in Planesville.

Eighty-five percent of the kids who graduated with me eventually finished college. In the class immediately before mine, nearly 90 percent completed college, and half went on to earn master's or law degrees (whose cost was left up to us to cover). More than two-thirds of the kids immediately following our class finished college. These college graduations occurred during an era when maybe a quarter of all high school graduates completed college. Not bad at all, especially when a number of the kids did not accept The Home's financial help.

College life eased the adjustment to the rest of the world for me. It was another *institution* with dorms, food lines, and laundry services, not unlike what we had at The Home. Dorm life never bothered me. Indeed, after a summer of living in a house with only one other person in it, who stayed to herself and said little, I was ready to move back into a dorm; I needed some noise around me. The only real problems I continued to have for a number of years were the small things that most people don't seem to sweat as much as I did. For example, I knew the basics about table manners (keep one hand in the lap and use your napkin), but trying to figure out which fork or glass to use when there were more than one was no small feat. And the number of forks (and spoons and glasses) rose through the years, as the dinners became more formal and the places for the dinners became classier. I hid the problem, as many others do, by never being the first to choose. I still feel like an observer when I go to expensive restaurants and clubs.

Mr. Shanes and Miss Winfield came to my college graduation, as they had to parents' day, when no one else did. Those things counted tremendously with me. I sent them both notices when I got my Ph.D. I could tell it was Mr. Shanes responding when I saw the envelope in my university mailbox addressed to "Dr. Dickie McKenzie." The department secretary got a good chuckle on seeing the envelope, which she could not resist hand-delivering.

Although we all left and went our separate ways, often distinguishing our ways from those of The Home, we are all frozen in time to each other by our shared experiences there. It's a nice thought that some things don't change. In my thoughts of how they—Dooley, CJ, and all the other boys and girls I grew up with—were back then, I feel a form of comfort, even warmth. Our lives extend back in time, converging in a place and a way of life few understand and many openly but wrongly disdain.

What we have done separately and collectively represents a commentary on what some pretty fine folks were able to accomplish with little. Mr. Shanes, who died shortly after he wrote me that letter, would be proud of us, but he would always want us to remember where we came from. Miss Winfield, who must be close to her centennial year and is frail from a stroke, must be gratified at how her life's work helped mold the future she imagined for us. I will never forget what they did.

II

FATHER TIME

OUR CHILDHOOD MEMORIES ARE AS UNRELIABLE AS THEY ARE selective, affected radically by the passing of time. Most good parents work hard at leaving their children with positive childhood memories. And children have a bias toward suppressing the bad ones and magnifying the good ones. I do have a few good memories of when I was very young. I remember a couple of happy family dinners in our small but neat white frame house in Raleigh. My father would delight in showing my brother and me how to eat steak smothered in A-1 sauce. Once he took my brother and me to see the great halfback Charlie "Choo-Choo" Justice play in a home game for North Carolina State College. And he used to give us the silver dollars he had saved. But in my case it's the bad memories that have stuck.

I remember being herded at the age of five by my mother into a taxi while my father was out of the house. She was escaping from years of physical and mental abuse. We took only what we could pack quickly into a few small suitcases. I remember all too well my father showing up in a rage at my aunt's house, where we stayed for a time, and my uncle trying to calm him down. My brother and I cowered in the back room, occasionally risking a peek at my father and uncle a hundred feet away, about to come to blows.

At the time, my father's behavior frightened and confused me. I now understand something of how he must have felt: his children were being taken away from him. I can now appreciate also the agony he felt, knowing that his in-laws were constantly telling his children how bad he was. He must have felt a personal misery deep inside that he couldn't let go, which drove him to drink. Our reaction — denial of his parental rights — must have compounded his internal strife.

My father grew up dirt-poor in the backwoods of peach country in North Carolina. I believe he was the only one of the five brothers in his family to finish high school, just possibly the first in the history of his family. Amazingly, he then managed — in the depth of the Great Depression — to gain a college degree in marketing from North Carolina State. That was an era when less than one-fourth of American students completed high school, and precious few men or women went on to college. It was a monumental feat at a time when many others like him were standing on soup lines.

Unfortunately, he wasn't able to put his college education to much use. He was always fighting off poverty, and had only four identifiable jobs (other than odd jobs) in his life. He first was a production worker in a wartime plant in Baltimore, then a railroad conductor for a short time after the war. For most of his adult working life, he was either a furnace repairman or, more often, a sign painter. He never had his own place of business (aside from a shed, which he built from scavenged wood and that stood at the side of his house). He traveled the backwoods of North Carolina, mostly in the area where he grew up, looking for signs to paint or repaint, mainly for the roadside fruit stands that ran through peach country. He was very good at it, too; he could paint letters and, if required, draw peaches as tall as he was without ever sketching them out beforehand.

On those rare occasions when I didn't spend the two-week summer vacations at The Home, I hated going to his house for two reasons. First, he would always drag my brother and me around the countryside with him on his search for work, and we would end up staying at some flea-bitten rooming house with all kinds of weird people prowling the hallways and bathrooms. But he proudly introduced us to his friends and anyone else who would stop and listen. Second, he was almost always drinking.

I don't ever remember my father sober past midday (except at my high school graduation). When we followed him on his painting jobs, he kept saying that he needed the beers to "steady my arm." By nighttime, he would have drunk himself to the point of muttering, if he could talk at all. He would then go off into wild harangues, laced with humor, about anything and everything—especially taxes. (Since he worked strictly on a cash basis, I doubt that he even paid taxes.) Given his constant drinking, it's a miracle that we never had a serious accident, although we did hit the gutters alongside the roads a few times.

He seemed to do everything in a stupor. When I was in high school, he called the principal and, with slurring words, demanded that he be allowed to see me right then (even though he might be hundreds of miles away), claiming to be from the "Office of the Governor." When I went to college, he called campus security to make similar demands.

He did the same when I went to graduate school and even after I began teaching at universities. When campus security called to say that someone had phoned with wild, nearly incomprehensible demands, I always knew it was my father, although I wished I could have been able to say, "I don't know anyone who would do that."

My father was the source of a great deal of pain and embarrassment in my life, and many times I wished he would just leave me alone. I wish *I* could have just left *him* alone, but I couldn't. Mr. Shanes more than once called me aside to remind me that he was my *father*. I remember one such private talk. The day after my father had pulled a gun on him, Mr. Shanes called me into his office to say somberly (he was almost always somber with me): "Dickie, you must remember that your father is your *father*. Nothing can change that. God teaches that we must respect our parents, no matter what. It may be hard, but failure to respect your father is not an option. 'Honor thy mother and thy father' — never forget those words. They come from God." The emphasis was always on the word *God*. Mr. Shanes's voice would go deeper as he strung the word out.

I tried my best to follow Mr. Shanes's admonition, most of

the time. The problem was that practically every time I would go to my father's house—especially after he would call claiming some emergency—he would be drunk. I don't mean that he had just had too much to drink. I mean that he would be totally wiped out, naked in his bed, wallowing in his own slobber and urine.

Toward the end of his life, in the early 1980s, I would sometimes see him when he was only half drunk. On those rare visits, after we made the mandatory walk to my father's booze store, we would often end up in his living room. I would remind him of what the doctors had said—"The drinking will kill you if you don't stop"—to which he would usually reply, "With all else that's wrong with me, do you think I need to worry?" (He had chronic problems with his heart, liver, and kidneys, topped off with ulcers and a slow-moving form of leukemia.) Then his face would become contorted in laughter. There wasn't much that he could not laugh about, from what the governor was reported to have said in the morning paper to some tale of woe from his youth. And he had a laugh that would echo through the neighborhood.

Not long after my mother's death, he had married a woman four years his junior, who, with only a few years of elementary school education, spent her fifty-year career closing the toes of hosiery in a turn-of-the-century mill within a stone's throw of their house. When I visited, she would often be cooking on the wood stove in the small kitchen. She cooked everything swimming in grease. She was warm and accepting of her place in life, but when my father got too boisterous, which was often, she was not afraid of reprimanding him in her high-pitched breaking voice, "Now, Mac, hush your mouth, you old fool" — which would bring on another round of laughter from my father and a shake of his head.

My stepmother would usually smile as she'd turn to me and say, "What's a person to do? Ain't never gonna listen to nobody, never." When he was not around, however, she remained his most unconditional supporter. She would remind me of how much my brother and I meant to him and how good he could be when he was not drunk, "Lord knows, your daddy talks about you all the time. Shows these pictures over there on the table to everyone. Tells everyone about you." And he *could* talk.

Nevertheless, on my visits, he always seemed to be drunk or about to get drunk. I would sit in his small dark living room on a beat-up, torn couch across from him. He'd be sitting deep in his overstuffed chair, hair (what little was left) white and pointing in all directions, many of his teeth missing (almost all of which he had pulled himself), body crumbling with the weight of his years, and eyes blue but with a pickled cast because of the endless spells of drinking.

He would eventually ramble, slurring his way through a number of subjects that had no connecting theme, his voice getting so loud that I worried neighbors would hear, even though they were hundreds of feet away. I would cringe when he would try to get my attention by calling me "Dickie-muck" or, worse yet, "Dickie-mickady-muck." He had called me those nicknames since the days of the white frame house in Raleigh.

He never understood what I did for a living. I remember he would always ask me, each time I sat with him, what I was doing and then how much I taught. In the early years of my career, I could tell him that I taught nine hours, to which he would respond in a booming voice, "Do you mean they make you teach nine hours a day?" "No, Dad," I'd explain; "it's nine hours a week." "A week!" he would always retort in disbelief (never recognizing that teaching required time for preparation). "Son, you've got it made. What the hell else do you do with your time?" a question posed always with a slurred chuckle.

I would then ask him how many hours a week *he* taught, to which he would respond, "None." Then I'd say, "Dad, you obviously have it made more than I do." We had that conversation over and over on different visits, and it always ended with a laugh. He surely would not believe my teaching load today. He would be the first to support any measure to cut my pay *and* his taxes.

I guess I continued to see him and to go through the same conversations partly as a chance to look over at him and wonder, Why? How is it that a person who had the drive to make it through college against great odds could end up the way he did? What was it that sent him off on the path that he took? Why could he never seem to get back on track, in spite of the huge penalties he had to pay? His life could have been so different. I could never find answers to my questions in his eyes, no matter how hard I tried. I don't think he realized where he was—at the bottom—or where he could have been.

Over the years I have often wondered where I would be if I had grown up with my father. Perhaps I should think of the question in terms of where I would *not* be. Suppose he had been a little less bad, a little more responsible—would he have gotten custody of us? Suppose someone had offered him a check to keep us—where would the money have gone and what would have happened to my brother and me?

I shudder at what the answers might be. I know that the decision to send my brother and me to The Home teetered in the balance of just how bad my father was, and that his being a little less bad might have made all the difference.

Because of his drinking, my father could not hold a job; he had to be self-employed. He could not, for many of his years, drive a car legally—his license had been suspended more than once—but he always had some rattletrap parked to the side of the house, which he claimed could beat any car at the local racetrack. He was arrested on a few occasions—once for resisting arrest, trying to fight off five patrolmen when caught driving drunk and without a license; he was proud it took five to subdue him!—and spent some time in a work camp.

He earned precious little income and was able to survive partly because of my stepmother, a wonderful woman who loved him and cared for him in her very meager house. He also got by because he took the welfare system for a ride. He died at the age of seventy-nine with less than five hundred dollars in the bank.

The message from my brother that our father was in critical condition that Saturday in June 1985 gave me pause, but did not panic me. I had received numerous similar calls over the years, all false alarms, a couple of them even my father's attempts to get us to come see him. I was not about to jump in the car and drive the two hundred miles from my home in

South Carolina without confirmation. Then, that evening, my brother left a second message, informing me that our father had died.

His death was not all that surprising, but my reaction to it was. In the hours after getting the second message, I felt a deep, unexpected sense of loss. His death seemed to mark the end of the past. It was, at least, a time of coming to grips with the past and of feeling a kind of forgiveness that was new to me. That night I stayed up late thinking a great deal about his life *and* mine, trying hard to sift through my memories of him to find some nuggets of truth that I could hold on to. In the early hours of the next day, I struggled to put down my thoughts and memories in a letter to my children. Writing helped me to remember and forgive.

June 17, 1985

Dear Children,

My father died last night. That's been an event that has caused me to reflect and to write this morning about his life. It is times like this that I wish you could have known him better. There is much about his life that prevented you from getting to know him as a grandfather or, for that matter, my getting to know him as a father. I could dwell here on the things that caused us to know him less than we would have liked, but those things don't seem to matter at this hour, and it is very early Sunday.

Let it suffice to say that there is something very poignant and descriptive about his death, coming, as it did, one day short of Father's Day.

He never had much. By our standards, he made his way through life in the lap of poverty. Over the past decade he had everything imaginable go wrong with him. He was sick most of the time, in the hospital much of the time, and probably at death had no organ that he could live without. He had to suffer his pains in a four-room house that had to be carefully heated in winter with wood and was never cool in the summer.

I suspect that his biggest worry in life was having enough wood to heat the house through winter. I say that because he always had enough wood neatly stacked in the back of the house to last several winters, or so it seemed to me. He proved that if you are poor, you don't have to be trashy in the way you stack your wood and keep your house.

He didn't have indoor plumbing until a decade ago and only installed an indoor toilet when the city required him to do so. The stove in the kitchen was wood, the walls were single boards running floor to ceiling, side by side. There were no doors between the rooms. The house, which sat on stacked bricks for a foundation, was old, small, but neat in a neighborhood that, at its best, can be described as dilapidated.

There is much that he didn't have. All of that doesn't seem to be important now. I write about it only to make the point and to tell you that what seems important at this moment is what he did have. In spite of it all, I can at this time never remember his complaining about what he didn't have. He marveled at the luxury I lived in, but it was all marvel, no envy toward me, my brother, or others. Instead, he bragged about what we had, what he could make with his hands, how he could still paint, make a shed from scrap wood. He worked hard at what he did, when he could work, was proud of what he could do, not what he couldn't. There is something to learn from the way he lived that part of his life.

In his last years, he was crippled with medical problems, and on those rare occasions I saw him, he would tell me about them. But he never complained like a lot of old people who have far fewer pains than he had. He could laugh about what his doctor could take out of him and still keep him ticking, and he could brag, again, about how he could take down his sons, how he fought Joe Louis in his early years in an exhibition match (which he truly believed he did), and how he gave the nurses at the hospital fits when he was in their care. There is much to be gained from a man who lived the way he was able to live from the simplest of means.

Oddly enough, I think he enjoyed living more than we ever will. He never stopped laughing and joking. And although he was always the assistant to the governor in so many of his jokes, he was always in them, the butt of them, and ready to enjoy them. There is much to be learned from someone who dared to call collect only to announce in his deepest of voices, "This is the governor speaking," an announcement always followed by an ear- splitting laugh.

I never knew him very well. There were times I wanted to very badly, but couldn't. I suppose I couldn't see him more often because of some memories that I could not shake, but I suppose it was also easy not to see him more. In the end what has counted

most over the years is that he was the one, the only one, who came
to my high school graduation. There were those who said they
were close and who said they cared, as evidenced in their sending
us to The Home, and repeatedly reminded me of how bad my
father was. But it was my Dad, not they, who saw me graduate.

In the end I know he was proud of me. In the end I know he
loved me. In the end I loved him very much. In the end I wish I
could have, would have, told him that one more time.

I leave this morning for his home to help my stepmother, but
more importantly to pay respect to a man who lived a long and
painful life largely camouflaged with humor, who taught me some
things about living I hope to make use of someday. There is much
that I would have liked to have changed about the way he lived,
but not the person he was at his core. That is a point worth
remembering on this Father's Day. I tell you this because he
might, just might, be listening.

> *With much love,*
> *Dad*

I believe that death is a marvelous time for the living in that
it forces us to find the good and set aside the bad in people
who were close to us, who made *us* possible. The eulogy forces
us to be positive. Death is also a time of forgiveness. It is a time
of renewal. It is a time for picking up the family mantle and
then moving on. Joe, the aging black man at the farms, used to
say all the time, "There is some good in everyone. You just have
to look harder in some cases than in others." He was absolutely
right.

12

HOMECOMING

HOMECOMING WEEKEND AT THE HOME, AS IT WAS ORGANIZED in the 1950s and before, was always a pretty big deal. In the week or so before, the kids in residence would be told to "bust butt" to make the campus shine. The grass would be cut with extra care, the bushes trimmed, all campus trash picked up, and the floors of the cottages cleaned and waxed.

Until The Home's football program was abandoned in the late 1950s, many alumni would arrive for the Friday afternoon on-campus game, so the stands would be overflowing with all the kids in attendance, old and young alumni, and members of the community and the extended Home family (including former and current staff members and their children). On Homecoming Friday, we typically played an opponent that could be soundly defeated, which allowed all team members to play. The prayers before the game given by the campus minister would always invoke the traditions of The Home, which were expected to continue far into the future.

The early arrivals would stay over for the much larger crowd that would attend the Sunday morning church service and the afternoon alumni meeting. All the while, many of us still in residence would mingle freely with the alumni, especially the younger ones, listening in some awe (and disbelief) to the stories they would tell about their days at The Home. To hear them talk, you might be fooled into believing they worked twice as long and hard as we did, which we knew could not possibly be true. They rarely talked of their defeats at football or basketball, which, they maintained, were few.

The importance of Homecoming gradually faded in the 1960s and 1970s with the loss of football, the cuts in the number of children in residence, and the change in administration and direction. Homecoming became mainly a church service and a noontime meal of barbecue sandwiches. The alumni news column in The Home's newsletter grew shorter. I lost interest and rarely returned in spite of living, for a time, in the same state.

In 1994, Ronnie told me things had improved and persuaded me to attend Homecoming. I had not been back to The Home for more than a decade. As soon as I got off the plane, I was met with a series of small surprises.

Of course, I expected a substantial change in vegetation, coming from a desert area of Southern California and landing in North Carolina, where the rain had recently been heavy. But I hadn't realized how tidy the city where I now live is (the medians of the streets are regularly mowed, the cut grass is bagged, and the edges are neatly trimmed) and how untidy the roadsides of the South can get, with the constant growth of weedy grasses.

I was also surprised at the contrast in income levels. Where I live, it is not unusual to pull up at a stoplight and be surrounded by five or six Mercedes (or equivalent cars). Back in rural North Carolina, where rusted and banged-up pickups are common, heads would turn if a Mercedes were to cruise by. I was surprised that I had forgotten where I had come from thirty-four years earlier. In my romanticized memories of the South, I had left out the trash on the side of the road, the broken-down cars in the side yards, and the empty gazes on so many of the faces.

North Carolina is supposed to be a rapidly developing state, but in the area immediately surrounding The Home, change has been gradual at best. Few new businesses have been added since I lived there. A number of storefronts in the small commercial area at the intersection of the two major streets of the town, a mile south of The Home, were empty, and much of the town seemed to be wasting away. The railroad tracks, which once ran through the middle of the town to The Home's campus and down which Conner and I took our memorable walk, had been pulled up.

The closer I got to The Home, though, I saw that most of the yards still looked neat, and that rocking chairs still stood motionless on just about every front porch. My stomach began to knot as I reached the edge of The Home's campus. The big red oaks in the middle of campus were still there, even more massive and towering. The old main office and a few other buildings were still standing, but most showed signs of having been neglected for years. Grass was growing through and breaking up many of the paved sidewalks.

The old dining hall with the bell tower in Georgian style had been replaced with a building that can only be described as uninspired, a cut-off brick box with white trim. Several of the cottages, including Larr's, had long since been torn down and replaced. Reba Gorman's Cottage was still on the hillside, but its top floor had been eliminated, turning it into an awful-looking structure (imagine a turn-of-the-century building with a flat-top haircut and a couple of massive air-conditioning units in full view on the flattened top). Every one of the Quads could have used a coat of paint. The weeds around them stood two feet tall in places where bushes used to grow. There was no order to the landscaping, just bushes here and there around the buildings.

The metal windows and trim on the old gym where I had religiously practiced my long shot were rusting away. The gym's front offices had been stuffed with junk, and it looked as though its windows had not been cleaned in ten years. Half of the venetian blinds on the gym's windows had broken loose from one end. The thick coat of dust on the court told a story of how long it had gone unused. The gym looked pathetic, but the Woman's Cottage was in even worse condition. Several screens on its windows were busted, its gutters were rusting, and its tall white front columns had curls of paint up and down their full lengths.

The farm on the east side of campus just behind the gym was, simply, gone. The harsh economics of agriculture and the changed direction of The Home had taken their toll. No fields or pastures were in view anywhere. Where the barns, mill, pig pens, and tractor sheds had stood, pine trees had been planted. Even the farm roads we had ridden to the field could no longer be found among the growing pine trees. Threatening "No Tres- passing" signs were everywhere.

The orchards had long since been replaced with pines. The dairy on the west side of campus was gone. Only the holding pen remained, and it was surrounded by—what else?—thirty- foot pines. Lord knows, someone must have gotten a deal on pine saplings.

The changes in themselves were sad. The evident lack of care everywhere was totally disheartening to me and the three hundred other alumni who returned that weekend to meet and greet one another with hugs and to remind each other of things as they once were.

I had come to Homecoming to take an extended walk to each and every corner of campus in hope of once again feeling the pulse of that life and drawing inspiration from the sights and sounds of campus life—mainly those of children running among the oaks and playing in the ball field. But there was no campus life. There were no children to be seen. No noise. The silence was staggering. On my way along the dirt road that once ran through the apple and peach orchard down to the old spring house, I was stopped by a burly security guard who had presumably been hired to thwart the growing damage to The Home's property by outsiders and the threat of damage by the children in residence. He apparently worried that I might be intent on vandalism, seemingly oblivious to the fact that it was Homecoming weekend.

I felt a deep sense of loss. I felt like an outsider, and cut my campus tour short. I drove up the highway to Planesville to join the other alumni, who would be staying at a local inn for the night. Even though I had not known many of the alumni who graduated long before I did, I could pick them out in the lobby and corridors of the inn. In ways I do not understand— some unspecified combination of demeanor and dress—I just knew who had grown up at The Home and who hadn't. I was back with my people.

A graying lady called to me from over my left shoulder, "Are you Dickie McKenzie?" and I knew I was home. I reintroduced myself as "Richard McKenzie" to people who didn't recognize me, but they would invariably respond, "Oh, Dickie!" By the same token, I knew others at homecoming by their Home names: Nose, Head, Dooley, CJ, Kize, Bird, and Slop-Bucket Joe. Time lost its forward flow that afternoon.

The Home, as I knew it, began to die in 1966 when Mr. Shanes left. He said he left because he wanted to spend the remaining years of his career in the pulpit. I suspect he wanted someone else to engineer the changes in The Home's mission that he knew he couldn't stop, and maybe didn't know whether he should.

By the time of Mr. Shanes's departure, I had been gone for six years and there were fewer than seventy-five children left. The board determined that The Home should shift gradually from helping hoards of disadvantaged children in permanent residence to serving the special needs of three dozen to four dozen severely troubled (socially and emotionally) children for short stays—usually a matter of months, rarely more than a couple of years. It would now take in wards of the court, or children who might end up in juvenile detention or psychiatric care. It would also make a more directed effort to rehabilitate the children's families. The social theory in the mid-1960s held that institutionalized care was to be avoided if—or, rather, whenever—minimal family care could be expected or foster care in a family setting could be substituted. Gradually, the funding from the Presbyterian church collapsed to practically nothing as The Home's religious program contracted. Reliance on public funding jumped.

As a consequence of the changes, The Home today takes in kids only after they have gone through a series of foster-care homes, have been on drugs, have gotten in trouble with the law, have been seriously abused in one way or another, or have undergone some sordid combination of all of the above. One child in the early 1980s had been in twenty-six foster-care homes before being placed in The Home. I don't know which is worse: abuse from neglectful parents or the abuse so often meted out by today's child-care system, which can be a form of social roulette.

The Home's children continued to attend the local public schools for a while. But in the early 1970s, area residents petitioned The Home's board and church sponsor to reestablish its on-campus school. The children, they said, were too disruptive—prone to fights and fits of violence. They were some of the first kids to pull knives on teachers (or so the word circulated at Homecoming).

Through all these changes, The Home has retained its name, mainly because of its considerable impact on donations. That

financial fact of life has required those of us who went through
The Home before the mid-1960s to explain to residents in the
area that we were there when conditions were radically different. We have had, in other words, to apologize for where we
grew up.

We also had to accept the fact that the administration in
1994 (it was changed in 1995) was a different breed, intent on
making its own institutional history. Only one person from the
administration came to any of the alumni gatherings that year.
We never saw any of the children who were in residence.

How strange to go back and *not* make connections with those
who worked and lived at The Home. How sad it was that the
administration was not able to see that the children in residence
might have gained something from talking with the alumni who
had proven that they could rise above their circumstances.

The most remarkable news of all came from one of the
alumni who sat on The Home's board of trustees: The Home
spends an average of more than $45,000 a year on each child!
That's close to twice the cost of attending Harvard University
for a year, and fifteen times the cost The Home incurred per
child per year when I went there in the early 1950s. Part of the
explanation for the high costs is that The Home now has one
and a half staff people for each child, a ratio that must be necessary given these children's behavior.

Moreover, when asked by a trustee what the children do in
the way of work, the executive director had a one-word answer:
"nothing." "Don't they mow the grass or help with the meals or
do some repairs?" "Oh, no," was his reply; "we can't afford to
pay them."

After checking into my room in Planesville, I retraced the

five miles back to The Home for a social on the lawn outside what used to be the print shop and is now a museum of sorts. The oldest person there was ninety-six, the youngest forty-eight. When I saw Dooley and CJ, I realized how old I must have looked. Dooley was graying only in his full beard, but CJ's face showed the weathering of more than his fifty-three years. He looked old. My white hair (which was light brown the last time they saw me) must have caught them just as much by surprise.

CJ had not lost his expansive Howdy Doody smile or his tendency to kid and tease. He called to me, "Is that Little Dickie, I mean Dickie McKenzie? I guess you don't hear that very often," and then let out a familiar roar of laughter.

Most of the girls I knew as sexy while at The Home had turned matronly. Only one or two had retained the full power of their youthful figures. Clare, CJ's sister, was still exceptionally good-looking. When I saw the girls—rather, middle-aged women—I was pleased to remember that a dance was scheduled that evening. I'd have a chance to dance a slow one with Clare, something I'd thought of doing many times over the years. (I got my dance, but, as these things always turn out, it wasn't quite the way I dreamed it would be.)

At that first gathering, we talked about many memories of The Home, mostly work, rules, and sex and mostly what we didn't do or couldn't do "back then." The girls stressed how they had been dedicated to keeping themselves and us pure in heart and body—but mainly because we all knew that any girl who got pregnant would be banished from The Home, and the next best alternative place to go was not very attractive.

CJ, who was always blunt, chimed in that "when we left The

Home, we had only one thing on our minds. Now, as we return, we're so old we can't remember what it was." When he left The Home, he said, he "had a twelve-year hard-on." Dooley confessed that he solved his abstinence problem the night he left: "I only hope that the gal I picked up that night did not have something that would only come to life after a forty-year hiatus. Thank God AIDS was not around then. I was not in a mood to discriminate."

We laughed a lot, as each person tried to top the other with some observation about life at The Home. One alum, Canton, reminded us about the times we spent cleaning out the central sewer. The crud would build up into a thick gray paste on top of the water, which could easily be mistaken for concrete. Apparently Ronnie made the mistake of stepping onto the "concrete" on one occasion and fell in up to his waist in waste. CJ added, "Yeah, my dog made the same mistake one time. He just jumped right in and went totally under," to which Dooley quipped without missing a beat, "That dog must have been a 'shit-su.'"

When I mentioned that I was writing this book, they could not have been more supportive (although they did not want their real names used). The general sentiment was, "It's about time." They understand that there are many untold stories and undisclosed sentiments about the way we grew up. They also understand the widespread misapprehensions about life in a home for children.

When I asked a stock question about how he wound up at The Home, CJ deadpanned: "Well, you see, my mother and father played the Parents' Game with me. They sent me off to school one morning, and when I returned, they had left, leaving me a note on the kitchen counter that said 'See if you can find us.' Of course, at the age of four, I wasn't very good at hide-and-seek on a national scale."

My "brothers and sisters of The Home" (and that is how much of what we said about each other began) would be the first to list the imperfections in our way of life. As John remarked, "Life at The Home was damn abnormal. There was probably no other place in the world like it. It was strange by the standards of the world outside. It was terribly confining. The Home was not a place where small children could find much affection. I did not know how to behave when I got out." However, we all agreed that it was *our* place.

In spite of the troubles, if there was a theme that ran through all the discussions it was *gratitude*, the kind that I have written about throughout this book. I was pleased to hear that the others also felt it.

I was taken aback at first with John's firm claim that The Home was "abnormal," so I pressed him, asking whether he would want to grow up there all over again, just the way he did. He didn't even let me finish my question before he popped in sincerely, "By golly, yes. On reflection, probably the best thing that ever happened to me is that my parents were killed when I was five. That may sound like a harsh thing to say, but we were miserably poor and my family life was terrible. I never— never—sat on a toilet before I came here. My children can thank their lucky stars that I grew up at The Home because they would not have had the advantages they have had if my parents had lived and I had not had the advantages I found at The Home."

The others chimed in with their own stories of how life at The Home had been difficult in many of the ways I've described, but it was, as Clare said, "one hell of a lot better than the next best alternative."

"God, were we restricted," she continued. "I spent more time in my room on detention than I think anywhere else for sneaking out, kissing boys, and doing the things girls want to do." Clare reminded me of the importance, from a romantic perspective, of the underpasses, especially the one on the north end of campus, close to the girls' cottages. It was there that they could do their "smooching" (as Clare put it) with their boyfriends, but even there they had to worry about being caught and having to spend time in their rooms. Clare told me how they often managed to get away with it: "one girl would stand at the top of the stairs of the underpass and keep a look out for the housemothers while I would have a few minutes alone with my boyfriend. You know, dating in the cottages could be no more than watching television with several other couples, and then we could not so much as put our arms around each other."

Does she have any regrets? "Not many," she said, citing the answer everyone else was giving. "What was the alternative? Remember, it was the 1950s, not the 1990s." Clare's grown daughter was listening to the conversation with a look of disbelief (but I guess that would be the case for most 1990s daughters of women who went through their formative years in the 1950s or earlier).

One person in the crowd was bending everyone's ears, as she had done at past Homecomings, brooding about how bad her life had been before The Home and, apparently, how much worse it got while she was there. Just about everyone at The Home had oppressed her, she told anyone who would listen.

She didn't get the positive reinforcement she needed. She confessed to being something of a basket case today, having spent the past half-dozen years in therapy, trying to cope with her bad memories and the defects that had been built into her psyche because of the way she had been treated during her childhood. She insisted that the rest of us were engaged in "denial."

Maybe so. We all have to wonder how many of the alumni who were not there did not return because they had lingering bad memories. Yet I had not gone back for a decade, and my reasons had nothing to do with regrets. They had everything to do with the fact that The Home had, for a time, no place for its past (it had only the name of its past), and I did not realize the extent to which the alumni themselves, not the place, make a reunion.

Suffice it to say that no one at the Homecoming doubted the validity of the one alumna's claims. She clearly had problems, and she was anguished. But, it must be stressed, practically everyone in attendance could say many of the same things. Many who listened to her rattle on told me later in private, as did Myles, now a successful investment adviser: "You know, I could tell you stories that are every bit as dreadful. I was a street urchin in Centralia before going to The Home at the age of five. But at some point everyone just has to accept the past. There is not a damn thing one can do about it. All anyone can do is do what can be done now. You can't constantly dredge up the past. If you do, it will cripple you."

CJ, as usual, was unwilling to mince words: "Let's face it, shit happens — to practically everyone, some more than others." A lot of shit had obviously happened to that woman, and it had obviously crippled her. For good and bad, The Home had a powerful impact on just about everyone who went there. The record wasn't perfect, but the group agreed that the record was pretty good. We knew only a few brothers and sisters who had been crippled by their experiences there.

One of the keys to our collective success can be found in something Dooley told me. Dooley has for forty years been haunted by what we did to the dog Lady. And his life since has been touched by tragedy: his ten-year-old son was run over by a car within a block of his house. But at Homecoming he reminded me: "There are a lot of people out there who have personal problems that are deeply troubling, but because the problems are inside and can't be seen, each troubled person feels he may be the only one in the world who suffers. People who grew up at The Home know better. We know that there are one hell of a lot of people who have problems. *We lived with them.*"

Neal mused about what it must be like for children who do not confront early childhood traumas. "Kids are resilient, to a degree. Tough times can toughen them. We surely were toughened by the things that happened to us before we came here and some of the things that happened here. I worry about young adults who live pristine childhoods, only to confront their first personal tragedy at, say, twenty-eight. I don't know whether they will have the resilience to recover, or even know how. Hell, by the time we hit our late twenties, most of us were pros at coping with difficulties. But then, maybe we are all fooling ourselves; maybe we are not as tough as we would like to think."

In my private conversations with Dooley and CJ, it became

clear to me that my reaction to Home life was at odds with the reaction of others in one important respect. One thing I know about myself is that I have a compulsion to drive ahead in my career, to achieve for no other purpose than to achieve, and I've often thought that is at least partially due to my experiences before and at The Home. But Dooley told me that he had the exact opposite reaction: "I've wanted to live comfortably, but I've never been ambitious. In fact, I'm probably the antithesis of ambition. I want the calm life, and I want to live life as best I can. That's all. My life's philosophy is, to the extent that I have one, 'Leave me the hell alone.'"

CJ said much the same. He had tried the corporate executive route, but couldn't take "kissing as many asses as I would have had to kiss in order to move up the ladder. I asked to be shifted to the manufacturing section of our company. There I can say and do exactly what I want. I am beholden to no one. And in five and a half years, I can kiss it all good-bye."

Dooley, who has been divorced for a number of years, told me something of his romances since his divorce. He said that after he has gone out with a woman several times, "she invariably says something to the effect that I'm different. Now I have a pat reaction: 'I know I'm different. I insist on it.' If I'm not different, I'll go out of my way to be different. My main advantage is that I simply don't have to work at it. In ways, The Home just made us all want to be different. It's a driving force in my life and, I suspect, the lives of many others here."

I suppose the reason I had such a wonderful time at Homecoming that year is that for the first time in a long time, I could be with three hundred people with whom I could talk virtually in code and be understood fully. Few conversations were ever

completed. Few points could ever be finalized without someone else jumping in. But, you know, not much had to be said.
It was great to be back at The Home, even if that place that
straddled the highway had been transformed. So had we.

The last thing I wanted to do on the Sunday morning of
Homecoming weekend was to sit through a church service, but
I did want to go to Little Gary's Chapel. Everyone would be
gathering there, more than had been at the dance the night
before.

The chapel is now rarely used for services, and that fact was
evident in the empty choir pews, except for one lone alumnus
who would sing an anthem at offering time. The service was
uneventful and unemotional—the usual routine of songs and
readings—until an older alumnus got up to make the roll call
of the brothers and sisters who had died in the past year. There
seemed to be a lot of names, reminding me that our era would
come to an end in not too many decades.

The person reading the names got choked up halfway
through, and my eyes went blurry. "At least," he said, "my name
will one day be read aloud to a group of people who care." But
the gatherings at The Home would end someday. There would
be no more names to be read, because there would be no more
alumni orphans. Who would be there to read the list with our
names on it? Who would be the last to offer a prayer for all
those who had gone before?

The minister for the day was a young fellow brought in for the
morning service because he was the son of a boy from The
Home. When it was time for the sermon, he got up in the pulpit
that towers over the congregation, ready to make his connection

with The Home: "I'm here this morning, I suppose, because I am a son of The Home. When I was growing up, I heard more Home stories than just about any young boy would care to hear."

You could sense the anticipation in the audience at what the minister might then say about life in The Home. But instead, he launched into a dry, witless sermon, no doubt pulled from his files, about stress and how it is the product of conflicts between our inner and outer selves.

After the service, I mentioned to one of the officers of the alumni association that they should have chosen one of us to give a talk that day about life at The Home, regardless of whether the person could wear the cloth, not someone recruited from outside for the job. She immediately said, "Maybe you could do it?"

If that invitation were ever tendered, what would I say? How could I capture what has been in my soul since the day I left? I know I would rise to the pulpit, look out over the congregation, shake my head with some disbelief written on my face, and say, with a smile extending from ear to ear: "Good morning, orphans!" To which I would expect them all to respond in unison and with a chuckle, "Good morning, orphan!" Then I'd begin:

I have never seen such a sorry-looking group in my life, but I have never seen one more beautiful.

Isn't it wonderful to be back Home and to be among people who understand who you were and, because of that knowledge, something of who you must have come to be? Isn't it wonderful to be back and tell stories that you never have to finish and, for that matter, can't finish without someone else butting in and finalizing the story in a way that doesn't fit your memory? Isn't it wonderful to be able to bring your sons and daughters and spouses and friends to show (not explain), with the sights and sounds of this group, why you are who and what you are? Isn't it wonderful to lie about the past, to exaggerate what you did while here, and have someone else try to top you?

May the word go out from this group that we are glad to be back—and to be together again.

I know that in this talk I am supposed to enlist the powers of the Almighty. Honestly, I don't think I can. He might, after all, question my sincerity. At the same time, if there is a God, He has worked His wonders in this group. You know that, too. He knows also that what He pulled off in this group was not easy. It took Him far more than seven days!

There are people in this country in very high places who maintain that the American Dream is dead. I don't doubt for a moment that they are wrong, wrong, wrong! I am standing before a group of people who know better, who know that they may not have achieved all the riches they deserve but who understand that they have lived one hell of a dream.

If there is one thing we all have noticed, it is that times have changed. The Home has changed—dramatically. If this were The Home of yesterday, the one we have all been talking about, the choir pews would be full. The paint on the walls of this sanctuary would not be peeling. The windows on the gymnasium would not be rusting. We would have painted the walls and scraped the rust from every window. We might have complained about doing those things, but we would have done them, and we rejoice this day about what we had to do back then.

We come back to this Home—our Home—not to lament the changes but to celebrate and reclaim our past. We have come here to reassert our own value in this world by claiming, in spite of what is often said to the contrary and in spite of the changes that have occurred, that the way we grew up was good—not perfect by any means, just good.

We know what Thomas Wolfe meant when he said, "You can't go home again." There is a sense of emptiness when we look at the walls of this church and the lack of campus life just beyond these walls. At the same time, few of us have ever been able to leave The Home we knew and came to love. We carry the memories of it and its people with us everywhere.

The place we knew has left us, but somehow, looking out over this group this morning, I get the feeling everyone here understands what I mean when I say that the people in this room will never follow suit. They will always be with us.

This weekend I rediscovered the special sense of family we all share. I hope one day my children will want to make the trip with me to see where I came from and with whom I made the trip of a lifetime.

Thank you from the bottom of my heart for going with me through all these years and for letting me go with you.

EPILOGUE

A FEW YEARS AGO, I WAS IN A DEBATE ABOUT POVERTY WITH A social worker in Chicago, someone who had spent many years in the trenches of the inner city. I tried to make the argument that many public relief efforts, while well intended, have simply failed. In his response, my opponent made two mistakes. He presumed that my arguments meant I was hostile toward the disadvantaged. And he tried to undermine my credibility by charging that I could not possibly speak for the disadvantaged in the country because I had obviously been born with a silver spoon in my mouth. I have tried never to allow my background to be part of my work, but that evening I could not help myself. I let go with both barrels.

The mistake my opponent made is no worse than the mistake many others make when they denounce the way my classmates and I grew up. For decades, child-care professionals have charged, with few qualifications, that orphanages "damaged"—emotionally, socially, economically—the children in their charge. The public has so accepted that view that *orphanage* and *orphan* have become the O-words, tags that are readily employed for political and ideological effect. This is regrettable for those of us who were there and for many children today who could benefit from the type of life-affirming experiences that can be provided by orphanages.

Indeed, the critics of orphanages would be amazed if they could see those "disadvantaged" children now. Dooley has spent many years working for the state's unemployment system in Planesville. He may not be the most well-adjusted person you could meet, but by what standard? The standard of the type of person he would have been had he not gone to The Home? He's done well for himself and is as fun-loving as ever.

Chandler did well at Phillips Exeter Academy his last two years of high school, but he came back to campus only once, and then with the airs of his newfound elite friends. I understand that he returned to North Carolina for college and then married into money. CJ has worked for nearly twenty-five years for the same North Carolina tobacco company. He has started his own nursery/landscaping business on the side, which he intends to expand once he retires from the corporate world. Conner went into the military after graduating from college, served for a time, and then left for parts unknown. No one can locate him. Wiley ended up in Wisconsin as a salesman of specialty plastics. My brother joined the army, rising swiftly to the rank of lieutenant colonel and retiring after twenty years.

Neal, who has both a master's and a law degree, has been the headmaster of several private schools. Last year, when The Home was seeking a new director, he asked to be considered but then withdrew the offer when it became clear that the board members had no understanding of the way The Home used to be and no inclination to return to its old mission. Rendall is in the business of revitalizing sinking hospitals and is constantly telling Home stories. You won't find a happier ex-orphan. Ronnie has sold his long-time optometry business and gone into the insurance industry (after a long, unexpected spell of unemployment). Rebecca keeps medical records, and Myles—who was several years ahead of CJ, Dooley, and me but who has aged more slowly than Dick Clark—advises clients on investments. Mooney is the executive vice president of a subsidiary of one of the nation's largest banks.

Several of the children who grew up at The Home before the 1950s went into the ministry, a couple took up farming, a number have their own businesses, and others have taken up the trades they learned at The Home: painting, plumbing, or carpentry. Almost all have made fine parents and many have become proud grandparents, and all the children of the children of The Home have heard their share of Home stories. From these descriptions, you can see that practically all of us have broken the supposedly unbreakable cycles of poverty, abuse, and neglect.

Interestingly, the boys I grew up with—even those who harbor bad feelings about The Home—all report that the power of their experiences at The Home has grown, not subsided, with time, perhaps because as time passes they can see more clearly the full length of the path that got them from there to here. My brother looks back with some anger and pain, but I don't believe he objects to having grown up the way he did, considering the alternative. When I told Dooley that I was writing this book and, in passing, mentioned Charles Dickens's writings on orphanages, he quipped, "It's interesting that you mentioned Dickens. I have my own way of putting The Home in perspective: 'It was the worst of times. It was the worst of times.'" Then he chuckled. He, like others, has a hard time dealing with some of his memories. He, like others, has a laundry list of things that he would have changed about the way The Home operated. I have my own lengthy list. But the great majority of us would not have traded it in for the alternative.

I am now past the half-century mark, and I'm more than just fine. I am happily remarried and have four terrific children (although the earlier divorce, one of my greatest regrets, left scars that won't go away.) I am not at the top of my profession, but I am far enough from the bottom not to have to apologize to anyone for my career record. I have taught at several colleges and universities that would not have admitted me as a freshman. And now, I enjoy a chaired professorship at a major university.

The path I've followed, surprisingly, did not seem all that difficult. I've worked hard, but the work I've done has always been easier than what I had to do back at The Home. I became a professor partly to ensure that I would not have to do the type of work I once had to do.

While my income is much greater than I could have imagined, income per se has never been a central motivation. I live far more modestly than I need to. I have continued my count of publications with religious fervor: I've published a couple of dozen books and hundreds of journal articles and commentaries—not too bad for someone who, at the time he left The Home, could not write or even read very well. Most important, I have the respect of professional colleagues and the approval of my students.

Yes, I have problems. I often wake up in the middle of the night in a panic. My nighttime breathing problem faded long ago, but nights remain a time to endure, with sleep broken at the slightest thought of a daytime problem. Christmas remains a moody season for me, as I try to cope with the joy others sense but I do not fully understand. But, on balance, I have been exceedingly fortunate and have little to complain about. I have been given the luxury of following my own drummer, although I fear that one of the lasting consequences of The Home is that the experience will not let me stop beating the drum, stop counting.

The Home was a saving grace for me because it changed my circumstances. But, if there is a central lesson here, it is that there is something inside each of us—call it a *will*, the capacity for purposeful, self-determined, and self-determining thought and action, totally independent of circumstances—that matters in what we do in life as much as, if not more than, circumstances themselves. The trick is tapping into that will and then turning it in the right direction.

A life course seems to me to be like an Easter egg hunt in

which the players don't know what the "eggs" are but they know they're out there. We must find the drive to look for them, and then to keep looking when others insist that all the eggs have been collected. At times, we may be playing against some pretty bad odds.

My path to modest success, the kind my seventh-grade teacher meant, was never clear to me while I was at The Home. I struck out in one direction and found some "eggs," recreated my circumstances, and moved on, always counting. Had I carefully looked at my circumstances, I probably would have thrown up my hands. If I did anything right, I *overestimated*, far beyond what was reasonable, what I could do, and acted accordingly. I accepted what amounts to the myth, repeated time and again at The Home, that we could do better than circumstances warranted. I was lucky to have others press the myth on me and then to help me make it a reality.

In late 1994, just after the Republicans won a landslide victory in the mid-term election and their leaders began to hint that they might propose bringing back orphanages as part of their welfare-reform package, I wrote a column for the *Wall Street Journal* in which I argued that privately run orphanages are a pretty good idea for some children. I was stunned by the depth of emotion that column evoked. "Successful orphans" wrote me from all over the country to say, "Right on!" They agreed that they had had a great life in their orphanages, which many of them also called "The Home." All of them gave their Homes credit for their successes. But the fate of my Home was typical of many. It closed its doors to children like me, leaving many stranded in horrific family circumstances or relegating them to the foster-care system.

The emerging crisis in child abuse and care will, I hope, force private institutions like The Home and those groups who support them to rethink their priorities. Child-care professionals will need to reassess what orphanages in a bygone era accomplished, and how they did it, and to discard their current obstinate view that family life is always superior to institutional care. Some institutions offer safe and constructive living environments that are reasonable, cost-effective improvements over what so many children now have.

I recently heard on the radio a nun who works at a children's home. In response to a reporter's question about the need to maintain families, she posed a few questions of her own, which I will paraphrase here: "By *family*, do we really want to include situations in which a mother ties her six-year-old daughter to the bedpost so she can go out to be drugged up? By *family*, do we mean to include situations in which a stepfather sexually abuses his stepdaughters, with the mother's knowledge? By *family*, do we mean to include foster parents who take in nineteen children to increase the size of their checks and then force the children, as young as two and four, to compete with the dogs for the only food in the house, which is the food in the dog dishes? We can't continue to believe that institutions are always inferior to family care."

Some of us who had tough young lives in the 1950s and before would be even more disadvantaged today. We would, no doubt, face problems that were uncommon in the 1950s, such as drugs. And those problems would likely be compounded by good intentions. Well-meaning people would try to keep us in our sordid family and neighborhood environments. If we were ever taken away from those environments, we would be returned as quickly as possible. We would not have the luxury of a sense of permanence. We would not be afforded the opportunity to chart a new life course in a radically different environment, protected from our past.

Today's disadvantaged children need a break. They need love and nurturing. When those precious advantages cannot be provided, children need, at a minimum, a safe, stable, structured, and permanent place that provides opportunities for personal growth, a chance to live down and away from the problems of their past. They need the break I was lucky enough to get at The Home.